This is my faith journey.

Nihil obstat:
    Rev. Timothy Hall,
    Censor librorum
    September 15, 2018

Imprimatur:
    †Most Rev. John M. Quinn,
    Bishop of Winona
    September 15, 2018

Cover, interior design, and composition by Laurie Nelson, Agápe Design Studios.

Copyediting by Karen Carter.

Graphic elements: © iStockphoto.com, © Adobe Stock

24 23 22 21 20 19   2 3 4 5 6 7 8 9

Our Sunday Visitor Publishing Division
Our Sunday Visitor, Inc.
200 Noll Plaza
Huntington, IN 46750
1-800-348-2440
www.osv.com

ISBN: 978-1-68192-532-5 (Inventory No. T2421)

LCCN: 2019951810

PRINTED IN THE UNITED STATES OF AMERICA

Acknowledgments

Scripture texts in this work are taken from the *NRSVCE Bible,* revised edition © 2010, 1991, 1986, 1970 Confraternity of Christian Doctrine, Washington, D.C. and are used by permission of the copyright owner. All Rights Reserved. No part of the *NRSVCE Bible* may be reproduced in any form without permission in writing from the copyright owner.

Quotes from the *Catechism of the Catholic Church* are taken from the English translation of the *Catechism of the Catholic Church* for the United States of America, 2nd ed. Copyright 1997 by United States Catholic Conference—Libreria Editrice Vaticana.

Journals for Catholic Women

Becoming Holy,
One Virtue at a Time

A Guide to Living the Theological and Cardinal Virtues

Sara Estabrooks

Dedication:

For my children, who teach me more about virtue than I could ever learn from any book. I love you. —Mom

Table of Contents

Introduction

Called to be Saints

Holiness is for saints.

You're probably imagining folded hands and halos on the heads of semi-transparent ethereal bodies. Maybe you're remembering stories of great deeds and heroic virtue. Perhaps the first thing that comes to mind is a holy card with a serene image of a long-dead nun.

But I'm not here to talk about that kind of saint. I'm here to talk about you. Are you afraid holiness isn't for you? Are you convinced you can't be a saint? You're wrong, my friend. God calls each of us to sainthood. Every one of us has a vocation to holiness. That may seem to be a daunting task, like it requires you to do something spectacular. It is. And it does.

But it's something ordinarily spectacular. Holiness isn't reserved for martyrs and world-influencers and historical figures. Holiness is for every woman in her daily workplace, every wife in the mundane moments of her marriage, every mom in the routine chaos of caring for her kids.

1

You don't have to leave your town or your home or even your kitchen to pursue holiness. You can practice it right where you are at this very moment. You can seek it in all the small tasks of your daily responsibilities. You can pursue sainthood in the place in life where you find yourself right now.

But how? It seems so hard! I want to be a saint, but I always fail.

That's okay. Don't get discouraged. Pick yourself back up and try again. The good news is you don't have to do it on your own. God will provide all the graces and tools you need. He will help you live a life of virtue.

A Life of Virtue

I first started studying virtue in earnest when I realized that "finding my vocation" didn't make me holy. That's right, my wedding day didn't magically transform me into the patient, meek, charitable person I thought it would. In fact, from that day on, things got a lot more difficult. Now I had not only my own weaknesses and shortcomings to deal with, but my husband's as well.

My vision of vocation was that it would make holiness easy. But that's not true for our particular vocations or the universal vocation to holiness. What I came to realize is that holiness is a fight. It's a journey. A skill. It takes prayer, dedication, motivation, practice, and, above all, the grace of God.

So I began researching the tools it would take to be a holy person—the virtues! Where do they come from? How do I get them? What would they look like in my life? Thankfully, the building blocks of virtue are instilled by God. So let's start there.

The Theological Virtues

The theological virtues, faith, hope, and love, are infused into our souls by God himself. They allow us to have a relationship with him. These virtues are the foundation of living a morally upright life.

Thanks be to God for giving us these virtues to jumpstart a life of pursuing holiness! But we have a responsibility to receive this gift and actively respond to it.

In the first part of this book, we'll dive into a study of Scripture that guides us through each of these theological virtues. We'll learn about the great gift they are, how to respond to that gift, and how to live the virtues of faith, hope, and love in order to grow stronger in our relationship with God as his beloved daughters.

The Cardinal Virtues

Then, for the next part of this study, we'll delve into the four cardinal virtues: prudence, justice, temperance, and fortitude. These virtues are pivotal in our quest for holiness. All other virtues arise from these key virtues and can be grouped to express their relationship to them. For example, humility arises from a sense of justice towards God, and chastity from temperance. Fortitude upholds us in the practice of all virtue, and prudence enables us to know and choose virtue at all times.

In each of these chapters, we'll explore biblical teachings and examples relating to these virtues, as well as take an introspective look at how these virtues can come to fruition in our daily lives.

#VirtueChallenge

A while after I got serious about my dedication to seeking virtue and pursuing a life of holiness, I began to share my journey in a supportive project on my blog (www.ToJesusSincerely.com) and social media called the "Virtue Challenge."

A friend once asked me, "How many virtues have you mastered since you began doing this?" The answer—none. Pursuing virtue is hard work. It takes constant daily effort, prayer, and practice. I haven't mastered much of anything, and I don't expect to on this side of heaven. But, by the grace of God, I've grown by steps, leaps and bounds, and tiny shuffles forward.

You see, holiness isn't just for holy cards and halos. It's not a still life picture of perfection. Holiness is for the person who marches her way forward every moment of this life, striving for heaven with all her might, with the grace of God to uphold her. It's for the woman who fights and falls and gets back up again. It's for the woman who never gives up in spite of all her shortcomings, because of her great love for God.

Holiness is for saints. And that means you.

I'm honored and blessed to have you join me on this search for holiness, this journey toward heaven. I pray that this book will draw you closer to Jesus and that, through the grace of God, you will be numbered among the ranks of saints someday in your eternal home, praising God for all the good he's done in and through your life.

Let's begin, shall we?

1: A Living Faith

Opening Prayer

My God, I believe. I believe in you. I believe in your power. I believe in your goodness, your love, and all the truths you have revealed. Thank you for giving me this gift of faith—for calling me to know you and believe in you.

I ask you to increase my faith. If there are any doubts in my heart, cast them out. If there are any questions, help me find peace and understanding. Any part of my heart that I have been holding back, I surrender it to you now. I open myself up to receive more fully the gift of faith you pour out upon me. You desire me to grow in faith; grant that I may never become stagnant. May I always increase in knowledge of you, belief in you, and trust in your plan for my life.

Lord, open my eyes to see how I can live my faith. Show me how to make my faith come fully alive in my life. Give me the graces I need to put my faith into action. I know that with just a mustard seed of faith, I can do great things in your name. Help my life be a witness to your power, your goodness, and your truth, which I hold so dear.

Through the gift of faith, bring the hope of salvation to fulfillment in my life. And grant that I may reach out to others, sharing the joy of faith with everyone I meet.

Lord, increase my faith.

Amen.

On My Heart

My heart goes out to our new student Riodam who just got diagnosed with a brain tumor. The prognoses doesn't look good - but you, my Lord can help this family. Heal him please - if it's your wish. Comfort them all through this journey. Guide his parents + family with your loving arms to help them all.

The Virtue of Faith

A Living Faith

Sam barreled down the hill, his worn out sneakers flopping on the hard pavement, red t-shirt with a giant image of the Eucharist flapping in the wind, singing "Immaculate Mary" at the top of his lungs. He was a high school student, discerning the seminary and on fire with his faith. Sam was the first person I encountered who was courageously, unapologetically Catholic. His faith defined not only what he believed, but also the way he talked, the clothes he wore, the things he did, and even the songs he sang.

I remember thinking, "I want to be like that." Sam was inspiring in the way he was not afraid to let his faith be visible in his life, even if that made him seem different or weird to others. I wanted my faith to define me and transform me like that. I wanted it to overflow my soul, to bubble out from every fiber in my body, just like his. *Be proud! Be visible!!*

The Gift of Believing

Faith, according to the *Catechism of the Catholic Church*, is "the theological virtue by which we believe in God and believe all that he has said and revealed to us" (*Catechism*, 1814). It's the first of the three theological virtues (which also include hope and love). These virtues "are infused by God into the souls of the faithful to make them capable of acting as his children and of meriting eternal life" (*Catechism*, 1813). Faith, our belief in God, is a gift. It's placed in our souls by God, without any help from us. But we can ask for this gift, we can pray to receive it, and we can help it grow.

Faith is infused in our souls, but it's not meant to stay contained there. We're not purely spiritual beings; rather, we're body-soul composites.

We can't separate the soul from the body, or else we die. In the same way, we can't separate the physical and spiritual aspects of our faith. We can't believe one way and act another. We need to allow faith to possess our entire being—body and soul. We need to let it shape our thoughts, words, and actions. We need to give faith rein over our hearts, our schedules, and our whole lives. When we do this, our faith becomes truly alive. It becomes a part of our personality, a defining aspect of who we are.

A Contagious Faith

A faith like that is contagious. Living faith makes others see us and say, "I want what you have." It inspires a thirst for the knowledge and love of Jesus, the Church, and the Truth. It spreads like wildfire to everyone we meet. They can't miss the fact that we believe in Jesus, we love him, and we live for him. At the very least, they are intrigued by the effect faith has on us.

The *Catechism* calls us to live the faith and to "profess it, confidently bear witness to it, and spread it" (*Catechism*, 1816). Making the faith contagious is our mission in life. Witnessing to our faith is not only a good thing to do, but also necessary for our salvation. It's part of our journey toward heaven. We don't have to be afraid of what others might think of us; God calls us to be confident in our belief in him.

Faith Lives in Charity

How does our faith come alive? How does it grow beyond internal belief to the point where it encompasses our entire being? In the *Catechism*, we read that "living faith 'work[s] through charity'" (Galatians 5:6, quoted in *Catechism*, 1814). Faith works through love. Our intense love for God inspires us to act on our belief in him. Our love for him calls us to proclaim his name to the world and to share the truth and the good news about our salvation in Jesus. It calls us to keep God in "God bless you," when someone sneezes, to pray grace before meals, and to offer to pray for people going through hard times.

Our love for others makes us want them to know God too. It casts out hesitation and fear when witnessing about Jesus. It strengthens us to be able to point others toward God with all our words and actions. Faith showers others with God's love—the love he first poured out on us. By spreading kindness and love to others, we can be untiring witnesses to the faith.

With love, the faith that was planted in our souls reaches its tender shoots into every aspect of our lives. It takes hold of our bodies and blossoms in a beautiful array of works. It inspires in us hospitality, generosity, and evangelization. It grows until it defines our very selves, until everything we think, say, and do reflects our faith. Every decision about what to wear, watch, or listen to is affected by faith.

I Want a Faith Like That

When we cultivate our faith with works of love, we will come to possess a joy that makes others say, "I want a faith like that." But when we have faith that visible, life won't be easy. There's always somebody ready and waiting to persecute the Church and her members. We will come across people who do not understand and people who may be downright hostile.

We might have our beliefs and choices questioned, challenged, or ridiculed. We may find ourselves in heated arguments with unbelievers. We could even lose friends and family over our insistence in adhering to the tenets of our faith.

But we must not lose heart. We must not back down. We cannot hide our faith under a basket in fear. As Jesus modeled, we must pick up the crosses laid before us and carry them down the hard road. Faith tells us that all the trials in our lives will lead to good in the end. The cross leads to the Resurrection.

Unapologetically Catholic

In this life, amid all the joys and trials that come our way, we're called to let our faith grow and shine. We're called to accept the gift of faith and share it with the world by the way we live, the things we say, and the works we do. With a flaming love for God, in whom we believe with every fiber of our being, we can be unapologetically Catholic.

We can lace up our worn out sneakers and don our Catholic t-shirts. We can barrel full speed down the road of life, racing toward heaven, proclaiming our faith at the top of our lungs with every word, action, and moment of our lives.

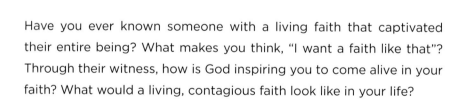

An Invitation to Ponder

Have you ever known someone with a living faith that captivated their entire being? What makes you think, "I want a faith like that"? Through their witness, how is God inspiring you to come alive in your faith? What would a living, contagious faith look like in your life?

_____

_____

_____

_____

_____

_____

_____

_____

_____

_____

_____

Connecting to Scripture

PRAYER TO THE HOLY SPIRIT BEFORE READING SCRIPTURE

Come, Holy Spirit. Fill me with every grace and blessing necessary to understand the message prepared for and awaiting me in the Scriptures. May I grow deeper in faith, in hope, and in love with Jesus as I spend this time with the Word of God. Amen.

✐ Matthew 17:15–20 _____

_____

_____

✐ Luke 22:31–34 _____

_____

_____

𝒯 John 20:1-8 _____

_____

_____

𝒯 Acts 3:16; 4:1-4 _____

_____

_____

𝒯 James 2:14-26 _____

_____

_____

_____

Scripture Reflection

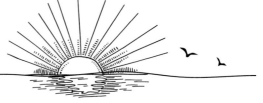

Faith Changes the World

Faith, works, and witness: they are intertwined. In the story that appears in Acts 3 and 4, we see how a living faith makes real change in the world. Peter and John came upon a lame man. He was a beggar and he hoped the apostles would give him money. But Peter and John gave him something even greater—they gave him healing in Jesus' name.

The crowd was amazed at Peter and John, but Peter was quick to give credit where credit was due. He told them this great work—this miracle—didn't occur by his own power, but that "the faith that is through *Jesus* has given him this perfect health in the presence of all of you" (Acts 3:16, emphasis added).

As soon as the beggar was healed, he began to praise God. He was converted on the spot. But the healed man wasn't the only one converted that day. While the crowd was wowing at the miracle, Peter got busy preaching about Jesus. He proclaimed the cross and Resurrection; he called the people to repentance. He taught, in no uncertain terms, that Jesus was the Christ. The Sadducees gave some serious pushback, but Peter wasn't afraid to shake things up with his faith. Because of this fearless witness, Peter and John wound up in jail, and the entire crowd—about 5,000 people—was converted!

Shaky Beginnings

Peter and the other apostles didn't always have a rocking faith like that. In Luke 22:31–34, we see that Jesus predicted Peter's denial and prayed that he'd remain strong in the faith even though he would waver. And he did waver. Peter denied Jesus not only once, but three times. In the end, though, thanks to the grace of God poured out on him, Peter turned back to the faith. He sought repentance, forgiveness, and renewed opportunities to proclaim his belief and love for Jesus.

In Matthew 17:15–20, we see another example of the apostles and their struggle with faith when they try and fail to cure an epileptic. Jesus had to step in and take over for them. He admonished them for their lack of faith. Jesus explained that it doesn't take much faith to move mountains, just a tiny mustard seed. But at the time, the apostles lacked even that.

We Believe in the Resurrection

What happened between then and the Book of Acts, when they began performing great healing and promoting widespread conversion? What change transformed the apostles from denying, powerless, cowardly men into miracle workers?

It was the Resurrection.

When Jesus rose from the dead, they "saw and believed" (John 20:8). Without the Resurrection, how would they have known that Jesus was anything more than another prophet or another martyr—another mere man who lived and died?

But Jesus rose again. He rose *by his own power*. This confirms that he is God. This is the miracle of all miracles that compels us to believe. The Resurrection is what gave the apostles surety. That was the bedrock of their preaching in every city and town.

It was the Resurrection that gave them the gift of living faith and the energy to act on that faith, though they still knew that it would be hard. Faith gave them the courage to go about preaching and healing, even though they would likely be arrested, imprisoned, and killed. Even death couldn't stop them, because their faith was a faith of Resurrection. It was a living faith. The apostles knew that Jesus had conquered death and sin and that they were called to deliver that message to the world.

Witness to the World

So they embarked on the mission of their life: to do great things through faith, in Jesus' name. They set off to be the miracle workers.

Their faith allowed them to do inspiring and miraculous works, and their works were a witness to the power of God. Through their living faith, the apostles brought about great change in the world.

But their goal never was to take credit for themselves. They always wanted to turn people back to Jesus. They wanted to pave the way to conversion. The fire of faith burning within them was meant to spread to others. God gave them the grace to endure hardships, persecutions, attacks, and rejection for the sake of his kingdom. Their hearts were set on leading others to Jesus, no matter the cost. The living faith of the apostles brought new life to the world.

Inspired to a Living Faith

God calls us to have a living faith too. When we ask through prayer, he will give us the gift of the virtue of faith, and the grace to make it an integral part of our lives. He will uphold us through all the trials of this life that tempt us to turn away from him. And he will help us spread the faith like wildfire throughout the world.

We can look toward the Resurrection and place our trust in the risen Jesus. We can know, surely, that Jesus is truly God, that he saves us from our sins, and that he loves us with an infinite love. And we can take this knowledge to our neighbor. Our lives can be a witness to his saving grace and power, every moment of every day. It can change the way we act, the way we look, and everything we do and say. By living the faith boldly and unapologetically, we can lead others to Jesus. Our faith, like the faith of the apostles, can be contagious. It can be a living, breathing, growing force that spreads throughout the world.

An Invitation to Share

1. Compare and contrast the apostles before and after the Resurrection. How do their words, actions, attitudes, and mannerisms reflect where they are in their journey of faith? Do you have a moment when the faith really came alive in your life, producing a before and after effect?

_____

_____

_____

_____

_____

_____

_____

_____

_____

_____

_____

2. James 2:14-26 states that faith without works is dead. In what ways do these other Bible passages support that assertion? How does this passage inspire you to put the faith into action in your life?

_____

_____

_____

_____

_____

_____

_____

_____

_____

_____

3. The *Catechism of the Catholic Church* says "living faith works through charity" (*Catechism*, 1814). In these Scripture passages, in what ways does the faith (or lack of faith) of the apostles affect their ability to love God and others? How can you see a similar effect of the virtue of faith in your life?

_____

_____

_____

_____

_____

_____

_____

_____

_____

_____

Closing Prayer

Dear Jesus, when you rose from the dead, you gave the gift of faith to the apostles. Today, through your resurrection, you continue to instill the gift of faith in your people throughout the world. You rose from the dead; you truly are the Son of God. Thank you for calling me to believe in you. Right now, I renew my resolve to respond to the gift of faith with my entire life. I desire to live every moment for you, who died and rose and gave every moment of your life for me.

Give me the grace to bring my faith to life through charity. Move me to act out of love for you, my God, and love for my neighbor. May everything I do show that I believe in you and love you with my whole heart. May my entire life point to you; when people look at me, may they see you, Jesus.

Give me the courage to endure any hardship that may come my way for the sake of my faith. Let me not be afraid of ridicule, persecution, or even death. Give me the strength, like that of the apostles, to endure all things with trust in your divine plan for my life.

Through untiring witness, may my faith open the doors of conversion to others. May it transform everyone I come in contact with and lead them closer to you.

Jesus, I ask you to make my faith a living faith. Let it shape my life: everything I believe, think, say, and do.

Lord, increase my faith. Amen.

Lord, increase my Faith

2: Unseen but Certain Hope

BECOMING HOLY: ONE VIRTUE AT A TIME

Opening Prayer

My God, all my hope is in you. In your infinite love, you saved me and opened the door to heaven for me. I know that salvation is a gift from you, and all I have to do is receive that gift. I hold on to the hope that no matter what, your grace is waiting to be poured out on me. Thank you for the gift of hope!

Lord, I desire to grow in the virtue of hope. Teach me what hope truly is, how it is a gift from you. Show me how to receive this gift, and reveal how it manifests itself in my life. Sometimes hope is a difficult virtue to hold on to; help me take an honest look at any obstacles to hope that exist in my life. Through your grace, may I persevere in hope even when life gets hard.

Give me inspiration as I study the virtue of Christian hope from the earliest days of the Church. Lead me with the example of your apostles. May I have hope in my salvation just as strongly as if I had been present when you walked on this earth, my Jesus.

I desire to live the virtue of hope. Give me the strength to embrace hope with my entire heart. Help me to accept my inheritance in your name and to put hope into practice through a life of joyful prayer and the fruits of the Spirit.

Lord, increase my hope. Amen.

On My Heart

The Virtue of Hope

Temporal Hope vs. Christian Hope

"I hope we make it there on time," I huffed as we pulled off the highway exit to make a U-turn. We were on our way to spend a day at the state park to get a big dose of nature. But instead of leading us to the great outdoors, the GPS was sending us right into the heart of New York City. There, it had a leisurely loop planned, before it would turn us around and redirect us to our original destination, adding an extra hour or more to our driving time. My hope was a goal based on my idea of a perfect day.

This kind of hope reflects the nature of our body; it focuses on the things of this world. It's good to have this kind of hope in our lives to keep us moving forward toward attaining our goals and accomplishing our daily work. But it can't be the only hope we have because this world will someday pass away. Since we're body-soul composites, we also need hope that will last forever. We need the virtue of Christian hope.

The Surety of Hope

Christian hope doesn't rely on the external circumstances we find ourselves in. Christian hope doesn't have an element of doubt. Christian hope is a sure thing. The *Catechism of the Catholic Church* describes the firmness of the nature of hope (as a virtue). It tells us hope is "sure and steadfast" and that it "does not disappoint" (*Catechism*, 1820). That's because Christian hope doesn't rely on our own strength or on outside circumstance to accomplish our goals. It puts our trust in Christ and leans on the Holy Spirit to give us strength (*Catechism*, 1817).

In life, we hope for many things: fair weather, fortunate circumstances, and favorable results to our latest workout routine or diet. But these are things that don't last. These goals exist in this temporary life we live on earth and require temporal hope. The *virtue* of hope looks beyond this world and this life. Christian hope holds God as its object. It's the "virtue by which we desire the kingdom of heaven and eternal life as our happiness" (*Catechism*, 1817).

And the good news is heaven has already been obtained for us! Jesus won our salvation by his passion, death, and resurrection. We don't have to earn it by our own merit, but simply *receive* it by loving God and doing his will (*Catechism*, 1821). We rely on the grace of Christ not only to secure our salvation but also to provide the graces required to demonstrate our love for him. He has won heaven for us, and he will help us "persevere 'to the end'" (*Catechism*, 1821).

With Jesus to lean on, we can stand strong in hope. We can keep our hearts on the things of heaven. All our actions and attitudes will reflect our sure knowledge of our salvation. Hope inspires us to live each moment with eternity in mind and produces joy in our everyday lives. It helps us know that the most important thing is heaven and that Jesus opened the doors of heaven to us. The things that happen to us now are an important part of our lives, but not the only part. They will pass away and seem like a blink of an eye when we enter into eternity.

Things, like being late to an event, getting behind on the chores, or failing spectacularly at our latest cooking endeavor, can't steal our hope and the joy it gives us. They're bumps in the road of this life, but they have no power over our eternal happiness. Instead, with the virtue of hope, we can look at these temporal disappointments as opportunities to embrace our salvation more fully by practicing virtue. Hope can reside in our souls in the midst of trials and disappointments (*Catechism*, 1818).

Obstacles to Hope

At times we can introduce or encounter obstacles that hinder our reception of the virtue of hope in our lives. If we sin gravely, we choose to cut ourselves off from God's grace and turn away from heaven in various degrees. We reject God's gift of salvation and the promise of heaven he holds out to us. Serious sin can make us feel anxiety over the prospect of eternal life in hell because it impedes our ability to receive the gift of heaven that God wants to give us. But the good news is that we can continue to have hope no matter how hopeless we may feel because God always desires to forgive our sins.

Another obstacle to our reception of hope is our preoccupation with the busyness of life. At times we can be so focused on the tasks and goals before us that we lose sight of our eternal goals. We give precedence to our to-do list and let our spiritual life slide. It can be tempting to allow chaos to crowd out God's grace in an effort to accomplish great things, and meanwhile forget that salvation is the greatest thing of all. By focusing on the things of this life, we can get distracted and begin to let our desire for heaven fade.

If depression and anxiety take hold in our lives, they can threaten to steal our hope too. Their grip on our minds and our health can cause us to doubt God's mercy and grace. They can introduce unfounded feelings of hopelessness and inadequacy. The devil uses these bodily ailments to attack our souls. Though temporal hope and the spiritual virtue of hope are different things that we discuss using the same word, the temporal and spiritual aspects of our lives aren't necessarily distinct. They come together to form the whole of who we are and often affect each other greatly.

When I suffered from undiagnosed depression, I encountered this struggle with hope. I thought that I was a bad wife, a bad mom, and a bad Christian. I had begun to lose sight of that assurance of heaven that gives meaning to life even in the midst of the greatest struggles and difficulties. It wasn't until I began treatment that I discovered how much influence the body and soul can have on each other. The physical ailment I suffered from the chemical imbalance in my brain affected my ability to receive, understand, and live the virtue of hope. I realized that depression (and anxiety) wasn't sinful, but that I needed help to begin healing my bodily infirmity so that my soul could once again embrace the virtue of hope.

U-Turn to Hope

With treatment, I started to be able to fight back against the clouding of hope that depression had brought into my life. I learned tools to help me cling to hope even when my mind struggled with dark days. Even when I didn't feel happy or joyful, I could still know for certain that my bodily health struggles didn't have an eternal effect on my salvation; life still had a purpose, and God still loved me with an infinite love.

We always have the option of fighting to overcome these obstacles to hope in our lives. Hope helps us persevere, even if we have to fight "to the end" (*Catechism*, 1821). It helps us redirect ourselves when anxiety, preoccupation, sin, or any other obstacles try to steal hope from our lives. Just like I had to redirect my GPS to pull a hard U-turn, taking me away from the heart of the city and back to my destination at the state park, sometimes our lives need a U-turn to redirect our eyes toward heaven and help us regain the virtue of hope.

We can turn to prayer to help us overcome the obstacles to hope (*Catechism*, 1820). Prayer is our way to express and nourish our hope in God. With it, we can cling to the promise of salvation held out to us by the merciful hands of Jesus. We can receive and rely on his graces to bring us to the eternal happiness of our heavenly home.

An Invitation to Ponder

How would you explain the difference between temporal hope and the virtue of Christian hope? When have you encountered obstacles to the virtue of hope? What steps can you take to overcome these obstacles and stand firm in accepting the gift of salvation and eternal happiness that God holds out to you?

_____

_____

_____

_____

_____

_____

_____

_____

_____

_____

Connecting to Scripture

PRAYER TO THE HOLY SPIRIT BEFORE READING SCRIPTURE

Come, Holy Spirit. Fill me with every grace and blessing necessary to understand the message prepared for and awaiting me in the Scriptures. May I grow deeper in faith, in hope, and in love with Jesus as I spend this time with the Word of God. Amen.

⌐ John 14:1–3 _____

_____

_____

⌐ Acts 1:6–11 _____

_____

_____

🕊 Romans 8:24-25 _____

_____

_____

_____

🕊 Romans 15:13 _____

_____

_____

🕊 Titus 3:4-7 _____

_____

_____

Scripture Reflection

Jesus: Watch This, Guys

Sometimes Jesus has a flair for the dramatic. In the Book of Acts, we see how he went to great lengths to set up an impressive Ascension scene for the apostles. Jesus took them up a mountain, gave a farewell speech, and was lifted up into the air and whisked out of sight by a cloud. While the apostles were standing by, mouths agape, staring at the sky in shock, Jesus had these angels pop in and chide them: "Why do you stand looking up toward heaven?" (Acts 1:11). It was a silly question, really. They had just witnessed Jesus' ascension; that's not something you see every day.

Heaven isn't literally up in the air, so this rising-to-the-sky scene wasn't necessary in order for Jesus to return to the Father. But Jesus' actions were necessary to make a strong point. This event prepared the apostles to receive the gift of hope.

By his resurrection, Jesus gave us the gift of Christian faith; by his ascension, Jesus gave us the gift of Christian hope. And we see our response to hope detailed in the images of the Ascension story. The apostles stood there with eyes raised to heaven. In hope, we keep our eyes raised toward heaven. Not our physical eyes, looking at the sky, but our spiritual eyes. The focus and goal of our life is the eternal: the things of God. The angels in the Bible help us see this connection. They cued the apostles to take their earthly eyes off the sky, but to lift their hearts and minds to spiritual heights: "This Jesus ... will come in the same way as you saw him go into heaven" (Acts 1:11).

Heirs in Hope

The angels' words also turn our thoughts to that bridge between heaven and earth: death, judgment, the second coming. When we think of these "last things," we can think of them in hope, not in sorrow or despair. Thoughts of death can naturally be scary and sad, but these emotions arise from the temporal aspect of our nature. They see death and judgment from an earthly view, marking *the end* of this life. But Jesus' resurrection and ascension show the opposite is true: death is a passage to a *new beginning*. It's the doorway to eternal life in our heavenly home.

Jesus pointed to this joyful hope of heaven back in the Gospel of John, when he foreshadowed the Ascension. He told his apostles he would leave, and that he would return again to fetch them and take them with him (John 14:1–3). John goes on to describe Jesus' promise that while he's away he will prepare a place for us in his Father's house. We are "heirs according to the hope of eternal life" (Titus 3:7). We are God's children, and he has a place in his heavenly home picked out, prepared, and ready for us. Just think of it: God our Father, preparing for our homecoming. Each one of us is his beloved child. When we die, we will enter into his home and receive our inheritance. I bet my room will be decorated with chic art, light curtains blowing in the breeze, a gorgeous view from the picture window, and a canopy bed piled high with feather-soft blankets and plump pillows. It's all metaphorically speaking, of course, but the point is God goes all out in his love for us and his enthusiasm to welcome us home. We can get excited as we look forward to the day when we will meet him face to face.

The Element of the Unseen

The Ascension reveals that Jesus went to heaven before us and promised to return for us, to bring us into our inheritance. But there's yet another important detail in the story that helps us understand why God doesn't just *show* us the awesomeness awaiting us: a cloud takes Jesus out of sight. In his letter to the Romans, Paul gives us a clue about this detail: "Now hope that is seen is not hope. For who hopes for what is seen? But if we hope for what we do not see, we wait for it with patience" (Romans 8:24–25). The element of the unseen is important to the virtue of hope. We can't hope for something that we see. We don't hope for what's right in front of us. Possessing something is the fulfillment of hope, and possession removes the need to continue hoping.

Rather, we hope for what is out of our sight that we desire to obtain. Here on earth, we can have our hope in heaven because it's unseen for now. But once we reach heaven, we no longer have need of the virtue of hope. Our hope is fulfilled.

Hope Expressed through Prayer

While we're here on earth, we need to practice the virtue of hope—we need to *do* something with it. As we read further along in the Ascension story in Acts, we see the apostles leave the mountain and join together in prayer (Acts 1:14). Prayer is the act by which we lift our minds and hearts to God. We express our hope through prayer. We also nourish hope with prayer, giving it fuel to remain strong and steadfast, and allowing it to enact the fruits of the Spirit in our lives.

Like the apostles, we look to the ascension of Jesus to give us hope. We are reminded of our heavenly destination and encouraged to keep our spiritual eyes on God. We don't lose heart by the fact that we can't see our destination. Instead, we have a deep desire for our, as yet unseen, personal salvation. With heaven on our hearts, we return to our daily tasks with constant prayer.

An Invitation to Share

1. Look for allusions to the Holy Spirit in the given Scripture passages related to hope. How do you think the virtue of hope enacts the fruits of the Holy Spirit (patience, peace, joy, charity, understanding, etc.)? What evidence is there for the relationship between hope and these fruits?

_____

_____

_____

_____

_____

_____

_____

_____

2. We are all heirs in hope, and Jesus goes before us to prepare a place for each of us in his Father's house. These phrases bring to mind strong familial sentiments relating to the Body of Christ. How do you think the virtue of hope inspires the biblical attitude of love for neighbor?

_____

_____

_____

_____

_____

_____

_____

_____

_____

_____

3. What obstacles to hope might the members of the early Church have encountered? How do you think they confronted those obstacles so as to persevere in hope? How does their example inspire you to fight to overcome the obstacles to hope in your own life?

Closing Prayer

Lord Jesus, sometimes I think life would be easier if you just showed yourself. If only you would appear, I could believe. If only you would talk to me, I could understand. If only you were walking beside me, I could know your will.

But without the element of the unseen, I would lack the virtue of hope. Lord, help me embrace your hiddenness. I don't see you face to face, but I see the world all around which you created for me. I don't hear your voice, but I know your Spirit moves in my heart to know and do your will. You don't walk beside me in human form, but you are always present to me in the form of bread and wine in the Eucharist.

Help me, when I experience your hidden presence, to look with hope on the day when you will be fully revealed to me. Give me the grace to keep my eyes on heaven. Help me have confidence in knowing that I'm an heir in hope, and that you have won salvation for me.

May I always persevere in hope. When I encounter obstacles to hope in my life, remind me to turn to you in prayer. Let that prayer cast out all fear and doubt, and return me to the surety in the hope I possess as a child of God.

By practicing the virtue of hope, may the fruits of the Spirit come alive in my life. May I radiate joy, peace, and patience as I look forward to eternal life in heaven.

Lord, increase my hope. Amen.

Lord, increase my Hope

3: Self-Sacrificing Love

Opening Prayer

Dear God, my Father, I love you. I love you for all the blessings you have given me and all the good you have done in my life. I love you for all the ways you have helped me in difficult times. I love you for creating me, for this beautiful world you have given me, and for life itself. I love you for redeeming me and saving me from my sins.

But above all, I love you because you are God and worthy of all my love. I love you because that's what you made me for and what you call me to.

Help me come to know you more so I may fall more in love with you. I want to be able to love you for your own sake because you thirst for my love. Help me grow in selfless love for you. Empty me of any desire for personal gain and any prideful reasons for my love.

As I grow in love for you, may I also grow in love for my neighbor. Help me love my neighbor as myself since that is what you desire for all your children.

Teach me how to make myself a gift of love for others like you did when you died on the cross for me. Show me what self-sacrificing love looks like and how to practice it in my life.

Lord, increase my love. Amen.

On My Heart

_____

_____

_____

_____

_____

_____

_____

_____

_____

_____

_____

_____

_____

The Virtue of Charity

Where's My Turn to Love?

I've sat down to write this chapter on charity who knows how many times now. Each time I successfully found a few moments to myself, someone suddenly needed my attention. Someone showed up to derail my train of thought.

When I set the alarm to get up early, my children decided to be early birds too. When I found a park bench in the sunshine, a lovely chatty lady sat beside me. When I poured myself a cup of tea after finishing my chores, an important phone call came in.

I really wanted to be annoyed with the people who kept interrupting my work. I wanted to tell them to please leave me alone; please go away so I can write about charity. But as soon as the thought entered my head, I realized just how backward it was. Would I rather write about charity than practice it?

So I put down my pen while I turned my love and attention to the people God placed in my life. As I looked at them, listened to them, and ministered to them, I realized what a misconstrued idea of charity I often have. I sometimes look at the big sufferings other people endure with great faith and love, and I wonder, When is it my turn? I've read about saints who accomplished great things in Jesus' name, and I ask, "Where's my chance?" I observe people changing lives by their charitable work, and I complain, "Why can't I change lives as they do?"

Heroic Love in Daily Life

I forget that big suffering and great accomplishments aren't the only ways to love. Behind every miracle or ministry or heartache is a story of daily life—a daily life lived with small acts of love for God. In my attempts to show my love in big ways, I forget that heroic love can be lived in small ways every day. I forget that love isn't about being recognized for what I do. Love is about God and my response to his invitation to unite myself to him in every moment of my life.

The *Catechism of the Catholic Church* defines Christian charity as the "virtue by which we love God above all things for his own sake, and our neighbor as ourselves for the love of God" (*Catechism*, 1822). We're called to love God because of who he is. God is love itself. Jesus revealed the Father's love for us, gave us this love, and asked us to imitate it by loving God in return and loving one another (*Catechism*, 1823).

Suffering is not a badge of love. Rather, it's the invitation to love. We learn from the example of Jesus that all suffering, great or small, calls us to die to self. But we shouldn't wait to be on the brink of death to show our love for God. We don't need to wait for persecution, illness, or martyrdom. The size of our adversity doesn't determine the size of our love.

A Living Martyrdom

Love acts in every small moment of suffering in daily life. It endures headaches, stubbed toes, and sleepless nights. It responds to a sink full of dishes and a floor that needs to be swept. Love sees past the annoyance of a bothersome neighbor or difficult coworker. Love is heroic in putting itself aside in little things in order to serve God and others. Our chance to love isn't some monumental event we're holding out for. Our chance is right now.

The martyrs each died to self in one great and glorious moment. But before that moment, they lived lives of great love for God and others in everyday ways. Like them, we have the opportunity to die to self in many small acts every day. We need to let go of the temptation to look for a grandiose opportunity that may never come. Instead, we're called to follow the examples of Christian martyrs by embracing a living martyrdom every moment of our lives.

When I find myself asking, "When's my time?" I remind myself that our time is now. Our turn has come. We can show God our love from the moment we get out of bed in the morning without hitting snooze to the moment we drift back off to sleep at night with one last murmured prayer trailing from our lips. We can show God our love from every phone call with a family member to every smile at a stranger. We can practice dying to self with each chore and every errand.

Who knows, maybe someday we'll be called to love God through great suffering, or maybe we never will. Perhaps we will love God with an endless offering of small crosses.

Love Right Now

Instead of waiting for our turn to prove our love with great suffering, we can answer God's call to love greatly right now. Though we may not be called to give all to him in martyrdom or persecution, we can serve God and our neighbor in little ways in our ordinary daily lives. We can give ourselves to him through a living martyrdom.

So now, I'm sitting here, awake past my bedtime, giving myself to God and others through pen and paper in this dimly lit room, though I'd rather be sleeping. But I don't regret it. I needed to learn about love before I could write about it. I needed to put my own goals aside and give myself to God's plan for teaching me to love him and my neighbor. I die to self a little bit right now, embracing the small suffering God chooses to send my way. I've grown in love a little bit and opened my eyes to recognize the countless opportunities to love him more and more.

Whether it's through a sacrifice of our time, our attention, or our attitude, we can heroically die to self in many small moments in order to make our lives a gift of love to God and others.

An Invitation to Ponder

When do you find yourself passing up small opportunities to love while waiting for your chance to show love in big ways? Make a list of some of the small (or big) crosses in your life. How can you respond to those crosses by sacrificing yourself in a living martyrdom of love for God and others?

Connecting to Scripture

PRAYER TO THE HOLY SPIRIT BEFORE READING SCRIPTURE

Come, Holy Spirit. Fill me with every grace and blessing necessary to understand the message prepared for and awaiting me in the Scriptures. May I grow deeper in faith, in hope, and in love with Jesus as I spend this time with the Word of God. Amen.

Matthew 22:35–39

John 13:1

1 John 3:16

1 John 4:7–21

⌇ 1 Corinthians 13:1–8, 13 _____

_____

_____

Scripture Reflection

God Is Love

Scripture shows us not only what love looks like, but what love is. It teaches us not just to do loving things, but to *be* loving. "God is love" (1 John 4:8). God isn't just good or kind to us; God loves us. God doesn't just love us, but he *is* love itself. Since God is an infinite and eternal being, his love is infinite and eternal. God chooses to give us the gift of his love—which, as the apostle John suggests, is the gift of *himself* poured out over us.

In his letter, Saint John goes on to call us to spread this love to each other. We love each other in the way God loves us, with the very love he gives us. We're not supposed to just be good or kind to each other; we don't give love simply by showing an emotion. We love each other with the gift of our very selves, by giving ourselves away.

Thinking of love this way can feel kind of abstract. But Scripture has many passages that teach us how to put this love into action. Back up to 1 John 3:16, "We *know love* by this, that he laid down his life for us—and we ought to lay down our lives for one another" (emphasis added). God doesn't sit around idly in love. His love is not some feeling out there. Too often, we think of love as the warm and fuzzies we get. But love isn't always pretty, and it's not sentimental.

Love Sacrifices

Love loves with sacrifice. It lays down its life for the beloved. This calls to mind Jesus' sacrifice on the cross. Jesus is God, who had the power to prevent his death but willingly chose to die out of love for us. He loved us so much he made the ultimate sacrifice of laying down his life to bring about our salvation.

This isn't some drama-laden Romeo-and-Juliet style love. We don't take our own lives in grandiose statements of love, misguided by unruly passions. Rather, we submit ourselves willingly to the suffering that comes our way, for the sake of the one we love. Dying for our beloved is the ultimate gift of self, but it's not the first or only one. We can lay down our lives in many smaller sacrifices of love every day.

In the Gospel of John, we see that Jesus' love was strong before he died on the cross: "Having loved his own who were in the world, he loved them to the end" (John 13:1). He didn't start loving us on the cross; the cross was the crowning point of his already flourishing love for us. Jesus loved throughout his life. He loved in every miracle, every healing, every sinner he forgave. He loved as he taught his disciples through lessons and stories. He loved as he fed crowds of hungry people. Jesus loved always, at every small moment, throughout his entire ministry. We don't need to wait for martyrdom—for life-or-death situations—to show our love. We can begin at any time.

The Gift of Self

Saint Paul, in his First Letter to the Corinthians, described how to love others through the gift of self in our daily lives:

> "Love is patient; love is kind; love is not envious or boastful or arrogant or rude. It does not insist on its own way; it is not irritable or resentful; it does not rejoice in wrongdoing, but rejoices in the truth. It bears all things, believes all things, hopes all things, endures all things." (1 Corinthians 13:4–7)

Each of these descriptions of love points to a way we can make a gift of self.

Love is patient. We can think of this not just as the passive act of waiting, but the active gift of letting go of our own timeline and expectations in order to serve the needs of others or accept God's will and timing. We don't just practice patience. We become patient. We let go of our impatience and frustration, and turn our attention to what God calls us to do in the waiting.

Love is not irritable, boastful, or rude. All of these attitudes stem from pride and selfishness. Love doesn't focus on pleasing itself or building itself up. It puts its focus on the other. Through practice, we can rid ourselves of the tendency to talk about ourselves, to build ourselves up, or to put others down. We can become the type of people who truly care about others, who want to make sure others know they are loved and worthy of love, and we want their good every bit as much as we want our own good. Love looks out for its neighbor.

Love bears and endures all things. It endures even death for the beloved, but it also endures every suffering that comes its way. It dies a thousand small daily deaths, even if it's never subjected to physical death. It offers up these sacrifices, and it doesn't begrudge them. Rather, we can look at our sufferings as a chance to offer up our very selves; to unite ourselves to Christ on the cross. Then our daily crosses are less of a burden and more of a doorway to love. They're an invitation to draw closer to Jesus.

Love believes and hopes all things. Faith and hope, as we have studied, direct our hearts toward God in this life and the next. We put them into practice through acts of love. Faith in the mysteries of God will fade away when we obtain full knowledge of God in heaven. Hope in our salvation will no longer be necessary when we attain it. But love remains forever: "The greatest of these is love" (1 Corinthians 13:13). Love is the greatest of the three theological virtues because the nature of love is infinite and eternal. Love will never fade away. If we love God in this life, we will be given the opportunity to live in love with him forever in heaven.

Love Endures Forever

God is love. Here on earth, we practice loving God and neighbor. In heaven, we will be face to face with God, who is love itself. We will live in an eternal relationship of loving him and being loved by him. The gift of love dies to self and, in dying, lives forever.

An Invitation to Share

1. Read 1 Corinthians 13:1–7 carefully, line by line. Try to let go of the idea of this passage as a checklist of the duties of love. Instead, reflect on this question: How does each "task" reveal the gift of self we're called to make in Christian charity?

_____

_____

_____

_____

_____

_____

_____

_____

_____

_____

_____

2. 1 John 4:7–21 is an intricate and detailed passage describing God's love. How does God's love enter the world and spread throughout it? What is the path of God's love, as described in this passage?

_____

_____

_____

_____

_____

_____

_____

_____

_____

_____

_____

3. In Matthew 22:34–39, Jesus was tested by a lawyer. Instead of con-
   forming himself to a legalistic view of obedience, Jesus elevated
   the Ten Commandments to be summarized as exercises in love.
   In your own words, how can you describe each of the Commandments with the mentality of "thou shalt love" God and neighbor?

_____

_____

_____

_____

_____

_____

_____

_____

_____

_____

_____

_____

Closing Prayer

Dear Jesus, help me to embrace the task of love in the little things you call me to. I've learned that great love doesn't necessarily mean seeking out great suffering or chasing great accomplishments.

*Great love can exist in every small moment in which I make myself a gift to you and others. Help me remember that love is not just about doing, but also about being. Inspire me to imitate the Father's love for me by **being** the face of love for others. Help me to practice patience, kindness, humility, and peace in an effort to focus less on serving myself and more on serving my neighbor.*

I want to rise to the challenge to love in the little things and to love right now. Don't let me sit around, waiting my whole life for my big opportunity to come. Open my eyes to see the countless opportunities you send me to love every day.

By your sacrifice on the cross, you show me the way to love. Help me imitate you by taking up my crosses—big and small—and following you. I want to make a sacrifice of my time, my talents, my desires, and my very self for love of you.

Lord, help me live a life defined by love. Help me love fully, by emptying myself of all selfishness, pride, irritability, impatience, and every other ugly vice that separates me from you and from my neighbor. Give me the gifts of compassion, peace, patience, sacrifice, and true charity.

Lord, increase my love. Amen.

Lord, increase my Love

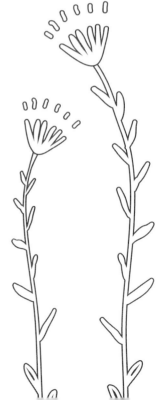

4: Prudence and the Rule of Life

BECOMING HOLY: ONE VIRTUE AT A TIME

Opening Prayer

My God, teach me how prudence calls me to step out and act confidently in a way that's pleasing to you. Sometimes I think of prudence as the virtue of staying away from the cliff or of being careful and timid. But while prudence helps me avoid wrong, it's not a virtue of fear or timidity. I want to do right by you, Lord. I want to choose what's good and follow your will in all things. Sometimes, this isn't easy or clear. Sometimes I'm even called to do that which I'd rather not.

Help me be more faithful to the virtue of prudence. Help me renew my resolve to seek what's right. Teach me how to discern which path of life you call me to. Guide me in knowing right from wrong, and in identifying the best of several choices. Show me how the virtue of prudence empowers me to live a full life.

Help me adhere to the standards prudence calls me to hold myself to as a child of God. I want to do more than discern and to know what's good for me; I want to desire it and choose it. Give me the strength to follow all the plans you have for me.

Lord, help me grow in the virtue of prudence, which enables me to choose and practice all other virtues. Help me set, and

even raise, the bar so that I may always choose to do what's best and most pleasing to you.

Amen.

On My Heart

The Virtue of Prudence

Knowing Right from Wrong

Eight-year-olds have the best insights into life. Our families had come together for a nature walk, and my friend's daughter, Lucy, stuck by my side like glue. As she skipped along, Lucy asked endless questions and bubbled an unbroken stream of adorable chatter. I don't remember most of what she said, but there was one thing I'll never forget: "Sometimes, I don't know I'm doing something wrong, but I get in trouble for it anyway." Her stream of consciousness quickly left this topic behind, but I never moved on.

How unfair she must believe it is, I thought, that she should be held responsible for actions she didn't know were wrong. But at the same time, Lucy had hit the age of reason; she was capable of knowing and choosing between right and wrong. She *should* be responsible for her moral choices, right? What's holding her back from being able to do that?

This young girl was trying to practice prudence—using reason to choose right—but her sense of right and wrong wasn't fully developed; her conscience still needed formation. Conscience is the voice inside the heart of each of us, encouraging us to do good and avoid evil (*Catechism*, 1777). At the initial level, conscience is guided by the interior law. This provides even children with the basic knowledge of right and wrong. But the interior law falls prey to things like "fear, selfishness and pride, resentment ... [and] complacency, born of human weakness and faults" (*Catechism*, 1784). The interior law could use some guidance in the practice of virtue. The conscience needs to be formed and educated. It's the task of a lifetime to continuously learn right from wrong and how to discern between good, better, and best.

Sometimes, knowing right from wrong can be tricky. Situations can be complicated, and we may not have all the information. A well-formed conscience is vital to guide us through these moments. But our conscience needs help from the Holy Spirit, the advice of trusted mentors, and practice in the virtue of prudence.

The Rule of Life

Religious orders often have a rule that determines the way its members live their lives. They take vows, or make promises before God, in the most important standards they hold dear. They have guidelines about what and when to pray, when to wake up in the morning, and when to go to bed at night. They answer to their superiors and often to a bell that calls them to prayer time or meal time.

Consecrated religious communities aren't the only people who follow a rule of life. Each one of us has a set of standards we live by, patterns or schedules we follow, priorities we live up to, and authorities we answer to. While our own rule of life might not be spelled out as clearly as a religious order, it's there, underlying, influencing every choice we make.

Prudence helps us establish a rule of life that sets good and holy expectations for all our behaviors and decisions. Prudence is "the virtue that disposes practical reason to discern our true good in every circumstance and to choose the right means of achieving it" (*Catechism*, 1806). It uses reason to guide the conscience in figuring out good and evil. But it doesn't stop with knowledge of right and wrong. Prudence puts that knowledge into action, doing its best to choose the good in all circumstances.

We're born with a sense of natural law, an innate basic knowledge of the rules of right and wrong. Natural law helps us do good in ordinary situations. We're bound by human law, reasonable codes of life that proper authorities require us to abide by. Human law helps us do good for the community by serving to protect the rights of our neighbor. But by the virtue of prudence, we're elevated to living under God's law. We're enabled to make the daily choices that serve the best good, our eternal good. Prudence establishes the personal rule of life we strive to follow, to speed us along the way to heaven.

Prudence sets the bar for practicing all the virtues. When we're tempted to gossip, prudence helps us speak charitably. When we're tempted to lust, prudence helps us act chastely. If we're caught up in the infinite scroll of social media, prudence enables us to walk away from our screens and put our time to better use.

It's a virtue that allows us to choose good over evil, and also to choose between good, better, and best. Ice cream is good to enjoy after dinner. But prudence may tell me it's better to serve myself a bowl of fruit instead. Prudence may even suggest I swap the snacking for fasting. It sets the bar and then raises it.

It's Not Always Simple

Choosing what's best isn't always simple. Let's take a look at some of the steps for practicing prudence. First, we encounter a situation where we realize we need to make a choice. It could be as simple as what to eat for lunch, or as serious as what vocation in life we're called to. We begin gathering information; we observe the world around us and learn about our choices. We open the fridge and scour the pantry. We learn about the Sacrament of Marriage and try our hand at dating, or read about and maybe even visit religious orders. We use our life experiences to evaluate the choices before us.

Then we look to qualified people for guidance and advice. We leaf through our cookbooks and browse Pinterest for recipes. We ask married couples and consecrated religious women to share their vocation stories. We humbly realize that the advice of others holds great value, and we let that form our discernment. We turn to the Holy Spirit for guidance. In matters with moral implications, we must not neglect prayer and heavenly aid.

These factors, when prayerfully considered, will move our heart toward a decision. We further double-check our heart with reason. This informs our conscience to know what choice is for our good. All that's left for the virtue of prudence is to move our will to action—to choose the good which we discern is right.

Prudence is a very personal virtue, and it leads each person to their own best option. Prudence may tell one woman to choose a salad with a side of protein for lunch. It may counsel another to add healthy fats or cut out carbs. It may call yet another to fast for self-mortification in reparation for sins. Prudence may lead one woman through the process of dating or courtship, to married life. Once she's tied the knot, prudence will help her choose to be faithful and loving to her spouse for life. Prudence may inspire another woman to give her heart entirely to God in consecrated religious life. It will help her follow the rules and practices of her order. Prudence may tell yet another woman that now is the time for her to make a great impact in the world through the career she chooses in her single life. It will guide and help her put her gifts and talents to work serving God's Church.

A Healthy, Holy, Prudent Life

In big and small matters and everything in between, prudence is the virtue that helps us discern and choose good for *ourselves*. Like eight-year-old Lucy, we might not always have enough knowledge, experience, or insight to make the best decision. But the rule of life established by prudence grows and evolves over years of experience and through the guidance of the Holy Spirit and trusted mentors. In all circumstances, we're called to use prudence to form and guide our conscience, and we are free, and even obligated, to follow the path our conscience directs us on. Prudence sets the bar for a healthy, holy lifestyle.

An Invitation to Ponder

Reflect on the rule of life the virtue of prudence calls you to. How have your life experiences helped you set the bar for your actions and choices? How have your choices changed over time as new knowledge was made available to you? In what areas does your conscience need further formation in order to act prudently? Does your rule of life need any adjusting?

Connecting to Scripture

PRAYER TO THE HOLY SPIRIT BEFORE READING SCRIPTURE

Come, Holy Spirit. Fill me with every grace and blessing necessary to understand the message prepared for and awaiting me in the Scriptures. May I grow deeper in faith, in hope, and in love with Jesus as I spend this time with the Word of God. Amen.

✑ Matthew 10:16, 19–20 _____

_____

_____

✑ Matthew 25:14–30 _____

_____

_____

✑ Luke 11:37—12:12 _____

_____

_____

✑ Luke 12:54–57 _____

_____

_____

✐ Proverbs 13:15–16

Scripture Reflection

Jesus, the Uncomfortable Truth

Throughout the Gospels, we often see Jesus preach against hypocrisy. In Luke, he called out some hypocrites who acted one way but felt a different way in their hearts. There were the Pharisees who closely followed the rules for show and love of self but were filled with wickedness inside. There were the scholars of the law who worked others to the bone without lifting a finger. There were the people who avoided sinners while refusing to acknowledge their own sinfulness (Luke 11:37—12:12).

These people set the bar low for themselves while holding others to unfair standards. They freely poured out judgment on others, even though they refrained from an honest judgment of their own actions. Many times, when these people interacted with Jesus, they didn't try to learn from him. They tried to trap him or to trick him into condoning their ways.

I see myself in them sometimes. It's easier for me to judge others and turn a blind eye to myself. I get caught up in the cycle of pointing fingers, but I don't want to admit I could do anything wrong. I let myself slide into familiar patterns of life, and I don't want to be bothered to change my ways to conform to the uncomfortable truth.

Jesus didn't pick on a few easy targets when he addressed the problem of hypocrisy. Later on in Luke, he chided entire crowds for their lack of judgment:

> He also said to the crowds, "When you see a cloud rising in the west, you immediately say, 'It is going to rain'; and so it happens. And when you see the south wind blowing, you say, 'There will be scorching heat'; and it happens. You hypocrites! You know how to interpret the appearance of earth and sky, but why do you not know how to interpret the present time? And why do you not judge for yourselves what is right?" (Luke 12:54–57)

The people could tell when the rain or wind or a heat wave was coming, but they couldn't tell that the Messiah was right in front of them. Their reason and right judgment were clouded. They cared more about popular opinion than personal discernment. But Jesus admonished them: "Judge for yourselves what is right."

Knowing Helps Choosing

So many times we can be like those hypocrites. We pride ourselves on having knowledge about the latest health trend, news story, or even the Gospel. We may even throw that knowledge in the face of others. We take pride in having all the right answers for everyone else but fail to take an introspective look at our own lives. The most important knowledge is knowledge of Jesus Christ. We may know the rules and laws of the Church. We may know the Bible inside and out. But do we know Jesus? Not just intellectual knowledge of him, but relational knowledge. Friendship with Jesus helps us live a full and abundant life. It guides us as we judge for ourselves what is right and wrong. It allows us to break free from the easy hypocrisy of creating a rule of life for everyone around us but not ourselves. It challenges us to take a look at the uncomfortable truth about ourselves: We aren't perfect. We don't always know the right answers about everything for everyone else.

But the more we know and love Jesus, the more we'll be able to grow in prudence, the ability to discern and choose what's right for ourselves. We'll be able to establish our own rule of life, rooted in seeking good and following him. The Scriptures have an abundance of passages on how prudence helps us choose good over evil. A quick leaf through the book of Proverbs will reveal countless sayings about the necessity of prudence in a virtuous life. But prudence helps us do more than just identify good and bad; it also helps us choose between good, better, and best.

Good, Better, and Best

Jesus helps us see the importance of distinguishing between good, better, and best with the parable of talents (Matthew 25:14–30). Two of the men who were given talents invested them, and the investment grew and earned interest. The third man, out of fear, hid his talent and returned it to the master as it had been given. None of these men did anything technically wrong, but it's clear that their choices had different values. The man who hid his money away until he returned it to his master "as is" could have done so much more. The man who invested his money and earned a lot of interest was rewarded. Jesus didn't hold back from qualifying these choices.

Like the men in the parable, we each have our own unique gifts and talents, given to us by God. Fear may try to convince us to hide our talents or tuck them away. It may tell us that our talents aren't good enough, that developing them is a waste of time, or that sharing them is the sin of pride. Fear tries to hold us back from living a full life with all the gifts God has given us. But prudence allows us to accept our gifts and talents as good. And even better, to nurture our God-given gifts. And best of all, to share those gifts with others to make the world a better place and give glory to God. Prudence gives us the freedom to invest in our talents as the men in the parable did. It helps us find fulfillment without being afraid of what others might think of our choices. Fear and timidity have no place in the virtue of prudence (*Catechism*, 1806).

A Life Well Lived

Jesus shows us that we don't have to be afraid of what others think about how we spend our time. Rather, with prudence, we can choose to invest time in our hobbies with a guilt-free conscience. We're free, and even obliged, to prudently choose what's good, better, and best for ourselves when it comes to developing our God-given talents. Jesus calls us to take the focus off of others and turn it toward ourselves. He challenges us to remove all hypocrisy and duplicity from our lives. With prudence, we let go of our desire to judge others and maintain our focus on judging what's right for ourselves. We form a rule of life that helps us seek a relationship with Jesus, do what's right, and choose the best option in all situations. Prudence establishes a life well lived.

An Invitation to Share

1. Jesus commands us to live wisely and innocently (Matthew 10:16, 19–20), and to avoid hypocrisy (Luke 11:37—12:12). Are there times when your actions contradict what's in your heart? In what ways do you overcomplicate things out of fear or concern of others' opinions? How can you take Jesus' words to heart, remove any duplicity in your life, and go back to simply seeking God's will in all things?

2. Are your opportunities to practice prudence most often choices between good and evil, or good, better, and best? Sometimes it becomes hard to see the importance of prudence in a society that promotes anything but moral certitude. How can you practice prudence in making the *best decisions for yourself* (Luke 12:57) in a world that values tolerance and mediocrity, and even holds an attitude of downright hostility (Matthew 10:16) to the things of God?

3. Do you prudently put your God-given gifts and talents to best use in your life? How can you let go of the fear that tempts you to hide your talents (Matt 25:14–30), and confidently invest in developing your gifts to fully be who God calls you to be?

Closing Prayer

My Jesus, teach me how to live life fully. Please help me to use prudence to develop a rule of life that helps me seek and do your will in all things. May I always base my choices on knowledge of you and in the discernment of your will. Don't let me be distracted by the opinions of others.

I want my heart to stay in the right place, focused on doing your will. Keep me from all hypocrisy and duplicity. Grant that my actions may always reflect what I know is right in my heart. And grant that my heart may always be guided by a well-formed conscience, grounded in right reason and knowledge of all that is good. May my life be lived in a constant quest to know and do what's right. As I grow in experience and knowledge of you, may my actions always reflect a renewed sense of wisdom and prudence.

Help me have gratitude for all the gifts and talents you've blessed me with. I long to use them for your glory. May I prudently invest in them and develop them—confidently, and without fear. I know that you have given me these gifts for my own good and happiness, and for your glory, my God.

Jesus, guide me to prudently set the bar that guides me to live life according to your will, and then help me raise the bar to seek a life that is ever more pleasing to you.

Amen.

Lord, help me choose to do what's best and most pleasing to you.

Prudence

5: Justice: Giving, Not Getting

BECOMING HOLY: ONE VIRTUE AT A TIME

Opening Prayer

My God, you are a just God. You give me all that I need and more. You created the world and everything in it for me, that I may flourish and live a full life. Everything I have I received as a gift from you, even my life itself.

Help me realize I owe you everything. Give me the desire to repay you through love. Inspire me to adore you, praise you, worship you, and honor you. I want to live my whole life as a gift to you because that's what you deserve. I desire true repentance for all the times I didn't love you as I should because you are worthy of all my love and obedience.

My God, show me how to imitate your justice in my actions and attitude toward my neighbor. May I always seek to serve others and meet their needs. Give me joy in sacrificing to make other people's lives better. Help me see the value and dignity of every life: from the smallest and youngest to the most esteemed, to the frail and elderly, and everyone in between.

I desire to learn how to think and behave with the virtue of justice. Guide my heart and inspire my actions to seek to give you all you deserve, my God, and to respond to the needs of my neighbor. Amen.

On My Heart

_____

_____

_____

_____

_____

_____

_____

_____

_____

_____

_____

_____

_____

_____

The Virtue of Justice

That's Not Fair

The students across the hall burst into raucous laughter, making every head in my classroom turn. My marker paused mid-equation, and my attention was drawn away from my own students to the scene next door. The teacher was rocked back in his chair, feet perched on the whiteboard tray, fantasy football stats displayed on his computer screen.

"What are they always doing over there?" I wondered aloud. My question was supposed to be rhetorical, but it was met with a chorus of answers from his former students.

"He just talks about sports all day."

"We never learned anything."

"All we ever did was standardized test prep."

I'm not one to judge teachers based on disgruntled students' remarks, but their description of his classroom matched everything I witnessed from my teacher's desk view. For the sake of professional respect, I cut off the remarks without comment and resumed my Algebra presentation. Meanwhile, Mr. Football continued to crack jokes and toss foam balls across his classroom.

Not many months later, we filed into the school auditorium for an end-of-the-year faculty meeting. Various unedifying speeches were made, and people I didn't recognize were applauded. I stifled a yawn and tried not to look too bored. Then the time came for the math teacher of the year award. I perked up, interested to know who it was. As a new teacher, finishing my first year, I was eager to learn from the best of the best, to gain insider tips and advice.

But whaddya know, it was Mr. Lazybones from across the hall. Apparently, he had killer standardized test success rates. While he sat behind his desk, making friends with the sports kids and passing out reams of self-check test prep worksheets, I had poured every ounce into fostering a love for math, understanding, and retention of difficult concepts. He sat back and catered to the test scores.

How was that fair? Where was the justice? Well, if he gets an award for sitting around making jokes all day, maybe I should do that too.

My half-hearted applause revealed that my sense of justice needed some refinement. I wanted to know what was in it for me. I wanted to take his recognition away to get the credit I deserved. I selfishly desired to lower my standards to make things fairer for myself. But that's not what justice is.

Give Your Life to God

"Justice is the moral virtue that consists in the constant and firm will to *give* their due to God and neighbor" (*Catechism*, 1807, emphasis added). Justice *gives*. It's not selfish. It doesn't try to steal; it doesn't try to get. Justice looks out for what others need and tries to help others get their due. According to the *Catechism of the Catholic Church*, justice has two components: justice toward God and justice toward neighbor.

Usually, when I put "God" and "justice" together in a sentence, I paint a fire and brimstone picture in my mind. You'd better bet God's going to punish those sinners. They're going to get what's coming to them when they enter their eternal rest.

Rarely do I think about acting justly toward God. But he made me. He gave me every blessing in my life, and even my very life itself. He keeps me in existence every single moment. If he stopped thinking about me for just one second, I would vanish into thin air—poof!— gone. My debt to him is infinite. I owe God every breath I take, every moment I live, every good thing I do because, without him, it would all be impossible. I owe him my whole life.

The virtue of justice prompts us to recognize this infinite debt and makes us zealous in our desire to repay it. It draws us to Mass every Sunday and holy day of obligation. It compels us to observe the required days of fasting. It moves our hearts to prayer and worship and upholds us in keeping God's commandments. We repay our debt to God with adoration, prayer, sacrifices, and the special promises and vows we offer him (see *Catechism*, 2095).

Justice is the "virtue of religion" (*Catechism*, 1807). It seeks a concrete way to dedicate its life to be a gift to God in return for all he has given us.

Bring Justice Home

Justice also seeks to give our neighbor their fair due. When I think of neighborly justice, I often think of either the judicial system—throwing bad guys in jail—or charity—helping the less fortunate to get what they need. But according to the *Catechism* (1807), justice shows no partiality to the poor (or the great). Though charitable giving is good and necessary, it doesn't check off the box on the virtue of justice. No, that's a virtue we need to practice toward every neighbor, starting with those closest to us, our family and friends.

I love that the *Catechism* also explains justice establishes *harmony* in relationships and promotes the common good (1807). How do we bring about this harmony? By looking out for each other, by "habitual right thinking and ... uprightness of ... conduct" (*Catechism*, 1807). We can have justice in our daily lives by looking out for the needs of those around us. We can ask ourselves, "How do I serve them?" Many times, I find that the peace in my home is disturbed by my own selfish thinking. Discord is sown by trying to get what I want, often at a cost to others. Justice seeks harmony. It helps me get what I need while looking out for the needs of others. Justice often calls me to sacrifice my wants to some degree for the good of others.

Justice helps me see my husband's stressful day when I'd rather throw a tantrum because he hasn't taken out the trash yet. It allows my uptight schedule-abiding personality to let go when a friend has to cancel plans at the last minute. Justice generously and joyfully wants to meet the needs of others.

Justice allows me to let go of jealousy and envy and be happy for the good of my neighbor. It gives me the strength to say goodbye to my bad attitude when the teacher across the hall gets an award and my work goes unnoticed. It helps me look past my pride and see that he's doing good work too; he's helping students pass the required standardized testing. And justice helps me maintain my own sense of purpose in my work—reward or no. It gives me the motivation to keep pouring my energy into serving my students to the best of my ability, in the way God called me because my students deserve that.

Justice Gives Freely

Justice doesn't need recognition. It makes a habit of serving God and others because that's the *right* thing to do. It helps us train our minds to think generously about our neighbors and their needs, giving them the benefit of the doubt in their actions.

Justice isn't a virtue of seeking rewards. It's a virtue of giving. With justice, we recognize our infinite debt toward God, and we look for ways our gifts, talents, and resources can help others meet their needs. We embrace our call to sacrifice. We give God all the honor, glory, praise, and worship he's due, and we look out for our neighbor. With justice, we can live in harmony with others and with God's plan for our lives.

An Invitation to Ponder

In what ways can you bring the virtue of justice into your daily life? How can you build more time into your day to give God his due through prayer and worship? How can you adjust your attitude and actions toward your neighbor and promote harmony between you? Think of some simple steps you can take to selflessly meet the needs of others.

Connecting to Scripture

PRAYER TO THE HOLY SPIRIT BEFORE READING SCRIPTURE

Come, Holy Spirit. Fill me with every grace and blessing necessary to understand the message prepared for and awaiting me in the Scriptures. May I grow deeper in faith, in hope, and in love with Jesus as I spend this time with the Word of God. Amen.

✐ Matthew 3:1–12 _____

_____

_____

✐ Matthew 20:1–16 _____

_____

_____

✐ Matthew 25:34–40 _____

_____

_____

✐ John 1:19–30; 3:25–30 _____

_____

_____

✐ Luke 18:9-14; 20:21-25 _____

_____

_____

Scripture Reflection

God's Idea of Justice

Sometimes I think if I were God, this world would look a whole lot different. Good people would never get sick. Children would never go hungry. Bad people would see a lot more lightning bolts from heaven. Justice would reign, but it wouldn't be a virtue because my idea of justice takes away choice. It doesn't leave any room for free will, and it doesn't see the whole picture.

In the Scriptures, Jesus teaches us about God's idea of justice. The justice that Jesus reveals to us is a lot more complex, intricate, and beautiful. It's not just a structure, but also a virtue. It allows us to choose with love and generosity, and it finds its purpose and fulfillment in eternity.

John the Baptist

Let's start with the story about John the Baptist. He was kind of a big deal. He drew the attention of crowds and kings with his radical ways and fiery teaching. In the Gospel of John, people started asking: Who are you? The Great Prophet? Elijah? *The Christ*? But John the Baptist denied all these claims. Instead of basking in his own glory, he proclaimed his unworthiness before God: "Among you stands one whom you do not know … I am not worthy to untie the thong of his sandal " (John 1:26–27). He could have taken all the praise for himself. But the virtue of justice inspired him to point all his gifts and talents toward God. John the Baptist recognized the debt of honor he owed to God and directed his followers to give God that honor too.

A few chapters later in the Gospel of John, we see Jesus start to steal the show. John the Baptist's followers saw that Jesus was doing that baptism thing too, and they brought it up with John: This guy is stealing your trademark move! But again, he gave God glory and honor where it was due: "He must increase, but I must decrease" (John 3:30). It brought him *joy* (see verse 29) to see people turning to Jesus and listening to his voice. He's a shining example of so many virtues, but his tireless efforts to turn people to God with repentance, honor, and worship speak volumes of his sense of justice. Poor John the Baptist, his earthly reward was a beheading. That's not how I would have ended the story (y'know, if I were God). But God's plan for John surely includes an eternity of bountiful rewards for his great virtue.

We can take a cue from John the Baptist. Like him, we can view our entire lives—all we have and are, everything we say and do, our very life itself—as a gift of infinite value from God. We can acknowledge our littleness before him and the infinite debt we owe him. We can focus our whole life on giving back to God. We can use all our gifts and talents for his glory—to praise and honor him. When people admire us, we can point them to him, the source of our existence. And we can look for every opportunity to give back to God through all the gifts he's given us.

The Workers in the Vineyard

Scripture also revolutionizes our understanding of justice toward our neighbor. Jesus tells a parable that can be difficult for us to swallow, the story of the workers in the vineyard (see Matthew 20:1–16). Starting first thing in the morning, the boss went out at three-hour intervals to hire men to work in his fields. When it came time to pay, the boss gave each of the workers the same exact compensation. The guys who were hired early in the morning started complaining: "That's not fair!" And I would be right there with them. It's *not* fair. The people who worked longer deserved more than the people who showed up at the end of the day. They *earned* more.

But the boss tells them to step off: "Am I not allowed to do what I choose with what belongs to me?" (Matthew 20:15). As long as the early risers received their just wage, it wasn't any of their business what the boss chose to do with the rest of his money. If he wanted to be generous to the rest of his workers, he had every right to. Those guys who worked all day allowed their hearts to become selfish. They wanted to get ahead of their neighbor. But the boss, he saw that everyone got what they needed. He paid a full day's wage to the early risers—as he rightly should—but he also recognized the needs of those who couldn't find work all day long till punch-out time. They still needed to go home and feed their families. They still had to put food on the table and clothes on their backs.

The boss wasn't so focused on fairness and earning a wage as much as he was focused on *giving* and providing for the needs of others. He wasn't bringing down the people who worked all day, but, rather, he was watching out for the common good.

We can obsess about getting ahead, like the early risers. Or we can step out of that selfish mentality and choose to see the needs of others.

Like the boss in this parable, we can help provide for others out of a sense of generosity and commitment to the common good. We can choose justice—making sure everyone gets what they need—over fairness—making sure everyone gets what they earned.

The Corporal Works of Mercy

Once our hearts are in the right place, how do we go about putting justice into practice? For that, Jesus gave us the corporal works of mercy, because justice and mercy go hand in hand.

In Matthew 25, Jesus presented a guide to justice: feed the hungry, give drink to the thirsty, clothe the naked, visit the sick and imprisoned. He said, "As you did it to one of the least of these who are members of my family, you did it to me" (Matthew 25:40). This doesn't simply mean giving to charity; that's a good thing, of course, and almsgiving is a necessary practice in the Christian life. But it's a step away from *living* the virtue. We're called to bring this virtue home into our daily lives.

Justice sees not only the needs of those in faraway places throughout the world, but also the needs of those closest to us. We can drop off a meal for an elderly neighbor or a new mom. We can bring a drink out to the garbage man or mail carrier. We can smile and chat with the grocery clerk or barista. We can serve our family joyfully, knowing the great value in devoting our time and talents to meeting their needs.

Justice doesn't command the world to operate in constant fairness. Rather, it gives us the opportunity to respond to the imbalance of the fallen world we live in. It calls us to recognize the needs of others and do what we can to meet them. Justice moves us to give freely both to our neighbor and to God. It requires our heart and calls us to put the virtue of justice into practice in our lives.

An Invitation to Share

1. Look at the accounts of John the Baptist in the Gospels of Matthew and John. John the Baptist was acutely aware of his littleness before God. By his example and preaching, he pointed to many ways to give God his due. Which of his acts of justice inspires you? How can you be more like John the Baptist in dedicating your life to giving back to God?

2. In the parable of the workers in the vineyard (Matthew 20:1–16), Jesus inspires us to leave behind the attitude of earning our due and to embrace the attitude of giving each person their due. When is this model of justice most difficult to embrace or practice? Where do you see the greatest need for this radical adjustment in the understanding of justice?

3. How can you put justice toward neighbor into practice by following the corporal works of mercy as laid out by Jesus in Matthew
25? And not just toward your global neighbor, but toward your
family, friends, coworkers, and those closest to you?

Closing Prayer

Lord Jesus, I don't want to get overly caught up in the idea of fairness and a system of rewards and merits. Help me understand the virtue of justice as a call to give.

I recognize my littleness before you; give me the desire to praise you for your greatness. I acknowledge the infinite debt I owe you; may I seek to repay it through prayer, adoration, worship, and sacrifice. Help me use the gifts and talents you have given me for your glory, and to point others to you. Like John the Baptist, may all my words and actions proclaim, "You must increase, I must decrease."

I desire to recognize the needs of my neighbor and seek to generously serve them. Help me let go of my selfish inclinations and pride. Instead, may I be steadfast in practicing the works of mercy so I may help achieve justice both in the world at large and in my family and communities.

Lord God, give me the grace to make the virtue of justice a habit so that my life may be characterized by constant right thinking. May my actions always foster harmony in my relationship with you and with my neighbor.

Amen.

Lord, help me
understand and live out
the virtue of

Justice

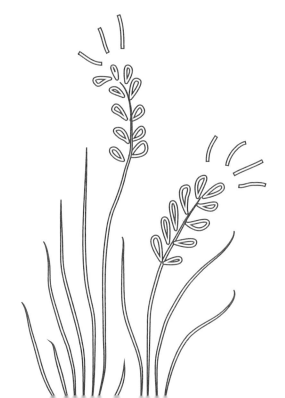

6: Temperance: Save Room for God

Opening Prayer

*God my Creator, thank you for making the world and everything in it **for me**. When I look around at all the good things you have given me—delicious food and drink, fantastic aromas, and beautiful landscapes—I know your love for me. You made all these things for me to enjoy. You are an amazing God!*

Sometimes, though, I'm tempted to love these things too much, for their own good. I fall into a habit of overindulgence of the senses. I seek food and sleep and pleasure as an end, and I get distracted from the most important things in life. I lose sight of the greatest pleasure of all—your love, my God—when I seek pleasure that passes away. The world tells me more is better, but the virtue of temperance tells me to moderate my appetites. It reminds me that there are healthy ways and unhealthy ways to enjoy created things.

Help me learn to use my senses to enjoy the things you created for me in a healthy way. May I always see them as a blessing, and give you thanks for your generosity. Help me have the self-control to practice moderation of my physical appetites. May my desires for the things of this world always remind me of the strongest desires deep in my heart—to love and be loved by you.

Dear God, help me grow in the virtue of temperance, so I may love you above all created goods.

Amen.

On My Heart

The Virtue of Temperance

Temperance Inspires Self-Control

"How are you eating?" Renee, my midwife, was concerned. I had three kids under four and was struggling to hold it all together. Admittedly, my diet revolved around cookies and chocolate. I had gotten into the habit of stuffing the quickest thing in my mouth to provide the calories I needed throughout the day. I was hooked on sugar and the easy energy it provided.

"I want you to remove added sugar from your diet," Renee counseled. Not limit, not cut back, but entirely give it up. Not only had I been swapping real food for junk food, but I had lost my taste for the natural sweetness of fruit—a healthy option. Renee knew it would be best for me to completely cut my ties with sugar in order to realign my appetite.

Temperance "is the moral virtue that moderates the attraction of pleasures and provides balance in the use of created goods" (*Catechism*, 1809). It's important that we start off with the fact that created things are good. But our fallen human nature can tempt us to desire these things too much. It can lead us to seek the pleasure they give in an inordinate and unhealthy way. Temperance helps us have self-control. It helps us experience the pleasure that we can with our senses, without overdoing it.

All Desires Point to God

All the desires we have point to our desire for God. We want to be happy, and our body shows that by seeking pleasure through eating, drinking, sleeping, reading, and relationship with others. But someday these things will all pass away. When we die, our souls will leave our bodies behind. Food won't have any more appeal to us. Sleep will no longer be necessary. We'll lack the senses our bodies provide until the resurrection at the end of time, when our bodies will be glorified and reunited to our souls.

But in the meantime, what pleasure will we have? How will we enjoy ourselves? In heaven, the greatest joy of all is to be in the presence of God—to love him and be loved by him. We need to learn to seek that joy while we're still here on earth. We need to learn to accept and receive his love.

Part of the way we do that is by receiving the gifts he has given us in this world. God gave us ice cream and chocolate—some of my favorite indulgences. It's good to have them occasionally as a treat, but God also gave us fruits and vegetables, meats, nuts, and grains. These things may not have the same appeal as sweets do, but they're better for our bodies and our overall health.

So there's a balance. Temperance calls us to learn to learn to enjoy the benefits of healthy food as our primary intake and to relish the occasional treat that sweets bring. It helps us avoid the temptation to overindulge on sugar in order to attain a greater good—health and wellness. It allows us to choose eggs instead of cookies for breakfast, in order to start our day out right. Sweets are good, but health is greater. There's a hierarchy that is evident in the consumption of food.

Moderation Seeks a Greater Good

This hierarchy points to something even greater than the goodness that food adds to our lives—that God is the greatest good of all. We desire the pleasure of taste and the benefits of health, but, above all, we have a hunger that food can't satisfy. We hunger for truth; we hunger for God.

Every day, we eat; and every day, we find ourselves hungry again. That's a void that can never be filled. That void can symbolize the void in our souls, which can only be filled by God. We should seek him as diligently as we seek our next meal or snack.

Sometimes the Church calls us to fast—offering the sacrifice of refraining from all or certain foods for a period of time, in order to offer penance and reconnect with God. We allow ourselves to feel the void, to experience hunger, and to remind ourselves that that hunger points to the greater spiritual desires we have.

Most often, when we talk about temperance, our focus is on food. But temperance is the virtue that moderates the appetites of all the senses. Temperance helps us seek and enjoy the benefits of sleep that revive and heal our body, and to avoid oversleeping, which can make us groggy and slow. Temperance moderates our consumption of alcohol. Alcohol is a good thing when used in moderation, in its proper time and place, but abuse of it is harmful for our bodies and souls. Temperance also moderates sexual desires. It's natural for humans to feel sexual attraction and to desire the union that it brings, but sex outside of the confines of marriage is harmful to ourselves and to society. Even within marriage, the sexual embrace must respect the dignity of both husband and wife. Temperance allows us to fully enjoy sex for the purposes God created it.

Too Much of a Good Thing

We can look at temperance not as taking pleasure away from us but helping us seek full and real happiness. Overindulgence in the appetites of the senses can be harmful to our bodies and our souls, and can actually diminish the enjoyment of the good things of life. Over-eating can result in unwanted extra weight, oversleeping in unwanted grogginess, over-drinking in unwanted hangovers. So we put this virtue into action to help us enjoy these things in moderation, thus avoiding some of the negative consequences that come along with "too much of a good thing."

It's not always easy to moderate our appetites. Eliminating sugar from my diet was one of the hardest things I needed to do—it required self-control in proportions that I'd never had to practice before. However, it was also one of the best things that I did for my health. It went a long way to helping me heal, forcing me to take care of myself, and allowing me to serve my family. Sometimes, when temperance is most difficult, a time of complete denial may be necessary—like it was for me. When I eliminated sugar, I found that I enjoyed fruits and vegetables more. They were sweet and pleasant to taste. I had missed out on that when my taste buds were so accustomed to the over-sweetness of constant processed sugary treats. After I reawakened my enjoyment of healthy food, I was able to enjoy my ice cream and chocolate again, in moderation this time.

Temperance also reminds us that all our bodily desires point to our greatest desire—for heaven. Everything we do in this life should help us on our way to heaven. It should aid us in seeking virtue and loving God above all else. Temperance keeps us from making false gods of things like food, sex, and even money. It reminds us that these things pass away and that we should seek the kingdom of God first.

An Invitation to Ponder

Think about some of the "created things" of this life that you most enjoy. How does your desire for these things point to a deeper desire for God? How can you practice self-control, moderating these things so that they don't take over your life? In what ways can you practice a greater appreciation for the goodness and blessing that these created things add to your life?

Connecting to Scripture

PRAYER TO THE HOLY SPIRIT BEFORE READING SCRIPTURE

Come, Holy Spirit. Fill me with every grace and blessing necessary to understand the message prepared for and awaiting me in the Scriptures. May I grow deeper in faith, in hope, and in love with Jesus as I spend this time with the Word of God. Amen.

🖎 John 4:7–15 _____

_____

_____

🖎 John 6:1–14, 22–35 _____

_____

_____

🖎 Luke 9:23–25 _____

_____

_____

🖎 Romans 8:12–14 _____

_____

_____

⌐ 1 Corinthians 9:24-25 _____

_____

_____

Scripture Reflection

Food: A Relatable Topic

Jesus had the truth, and he knew how to deliver it. The average person doesn't spend their days reading dense, technical theology. We prefer to learn through something more relatable: stories, analogies, and metaphors. Jesus modeled this by delivering theology through parables, imagery, and memorable descriptions.

Everyone can relate to the topic of food. When it comes to the topic of temperance, the first thing we need to understand is that food is good. Jesus showed us this over and over again by his numerous stories about food.

Living Water: The Woman at the Well

Some of my favorite food references are the ones he makes about himself. First, there's the incident when Jesus talked to the woman at the well. It unfolds in the Gospel of John, by the side of the road, in the heat of the day. Jesus had been traveling, and he was dusty and thirsty and tired. He came up to a well and plopped himself down beside it. Along came a Samaritan woman, and he asked her for a drink of water.

"Who, me?" she questioned him. They had a little back and forth conversation, in which Jesus was clearly teasing out some sort of lesson. The poor flabbergasted woman had no clue about who Jesus was and was rightfully confused by some of the things he said. Finally, Jesus threw this bold statement out: "Everyone who drinks of this water will be thirsty again, but those who drink of the water that I will give them will never be thirsty. The water that I will give will become in them a spring of water gushing up to eternal life" (John 4:13–14).

The woman was so excited that she would never have to do the tedious work of hauling water to her home again. She requested that Jesus give her this water. Instead, Jesus seemed to change the subject. He began to ask her about her husband. Then he began to tell her about her five husbands. Finally, it clicked: this man was a prophet, not just some random thirsty traveler. The woman realized that Jesus was the promised Messiah, that he was the one who could satisfy the thirst for love and belonging that she had sought through her five husbands. He was the one who could satisfy her need to be known.

This story started with the point that water is a good and necessary part of life. Jesus was thirsty and needed a drink. He used the opportunity to create a sense of community. Thirst is a natural part of life we all experience, and it's good to gather as friends around the comfort of drink. Temperance reminds us that food and drink are good and that they have their rightful place in life. But as this story unfolds, we're pointed to a greater good. Jesus revealed the woman's thirst to be known and loved, and ultimately, her thirst for God. We all have that desire within us. We can turn to humans for companionship, but we will never be fulfilled until we turn our hearts to God, the source of all love.

Temperance moderates the appetite of thirst. It reminds us that our body thirsts for things that pass away, but our soul thirsts for love that will last forever. Our thirst for water can be a tangible reminder to keep our hearts pointed toward God, for only he can truly satisfy. When we drink from the water that Jesus gives us, we'll never be thirsty again.

The Bread of Life

In John 6, Jesus had another great opportunity to use the desires of our senses to remind us of our spiritual desires. One sunny afternoon, Jesus and his apostles headed up into the hills to sit down and take a little rest. No sooner had they sat down than Jesus looked up and saw that thousands of people had followed them, and lunchtime was rolling around. Jesus asked the apostles to figure out how to feed them, and all they could come up with was five loaves of bread and two fish. Jesus proceeded to bless the food, and then he pulled off the miracle of multiplying it so that all five thousand people had enough to eat— and then some. The people were set on making Jesus king then and there, so he and the apostles made themselves scarce.

The next day, the crowds were at it again. They found Jesus and the apostles, even though they had retreated to the other side of the sea. Jesus knew they were looking for more bread. He told them, "Very truly, I tell you, you are looking for me, not because you saw signs, but because you ate your fill of the loaves. Do not work for the food that perishes, but for the food that endures for eternal life, which the Son of Man will give you" (John 6:26–27). The point is not that food is bad. If that were it, Jesus wouldn't have fed them in the first place. Food is a good thing; so Jesus made sure they had enough—no, *more* than enough.

But food isn't everything. No matter how much we eat, hunger will always return. Once again, Jesus used the example of bodily desires to point to spiritual desires. We hunger for fulfillment and purpose in life. We long for a meaning that surpasses the cycle of eating and being hungry again. We long for more than temporary fulfillment. We desire something that will never pass away—we desire heaven.

Jesus not only gives us the promise of heaven but an actual taste of heaven when he says, "I am the bread of life" (John 6: 35). Jesus' most difficult teaching to accept is the Eucharist—we are called to consume him, to eat his flesh and drink his blood. When he comes to us in the Eucharist, we receive all of him: body, blood, soul, and divinity.

The connection is so strong that Jesus doesn't stop at a metaphor with this one. He changes the substance of the bread into his actual self—food that will truly nourish our souls and help us attain heaven. Food is good, bread is great, but the best thing of all is to remind ourselves that our hunger for food can never fully be satisfied. We shouldn't focus so much on food that perishes that we lose sight of the food that lasts forever. We should let our bodily hunger remind us to seek heaven above all things and to feed our souls by frequent reception of the Eucharist.

Temperance: Save Room for God

Jesus' food analogies, his parables, his miracles and teachings, and ultimately, his gift of himself as our food in the Sacrament of the Eucharist teach us about the purpose behind the virtue of temperance. Temperance isn't necessary because food is bad. Temperance is a virtue that reminds us that our bodily appetites point to something more. They point to our spiritual appetites, our desire for heaven. Just like we make sure to save room for dessert by practicing self-restraint at dinnertime, temperance helps us moderate the desires of our senses, practicing self-control in order to save room for God.

An Invitation to Share

1. When Jesus promises living water and calls himself the bread of life, do you think he's minimizing the value of food and drink, confirming it, or elevating it? How does this impact the way you view what you eat and drink?

_____

_____

_____

_____

_____

_____

_____

_____

_____

_____

_____

_____

_____

2. The two stories in this reflection focus on moderating the sense of taste. How can you apply the wisdom of these stories to temperance of the other senses? In what ways can our desires relating to sight, hearing, touch, and smell point to our desire for God?

3. In Luke 9:23-25 and 1 Corinthians 9:24-25, the Scriptures talk about how self-denial in material things helps attain spiritual goals. In what ways do these verses inspire you to make sacrifices in seeking pleasure from your senses in order to attain greater spiritual good?

Closing Prayer

My Jesus, by becoming human and sharing my experience of the senses, you showed me that the material world isn't a bad thing. Food, drink, sleep, relaxation, and enjoyment of the things of this world are all good. You reminded me of the goodness of created things by eating and drinking, by multiplying bread and fish to feed the hungry, and by your many stories and parables relating to food and drink.

But you also remind me that my desire for the pleasures of this world point to my desire for the things of God. I will eat and be hungry again; I will drink and be thirsty again. My deepest hunger will never be satisfied by bread; I hunger for your love. My strongest thirst will never be satisfied with water; I thirst for your spirit and truth.

Open my heart to see how the desires for food, drink, and the other good things of this world point my heart toward you. Help me to seek you above all the things you created for me. May my enjoyment of created things always remind me of your goodness, and point my heart back to you.

Help me to deny myself of earthly pleasure from time to time, in order to make room to love you more. I want to take up the cross you call me to carry in this life, so that I may share in your divine life in heaven.

Jesus, give me temperance, that my heart may have room to love you most of all.

Amen.

Lord, help me
grow in
Temperance

7: Fortitude: Holy Courage

BECOMING HOLY: ONE VIRTUE AT A TIME

Opening Prayer

Dear God, life can be so hard. When challenges and difficulties come my way, I'm tempted to hide. When crosses and heartaches present themselves, I feel like running away. When fear and anxiety grip me, I want to close my eyes and make it all disappear. Sometimes I want to withdraw into my own personal bubble to hide from the hardships this life brings.

When I want to hide, my God, you call me forth. You beckon me to step out in fortitude. You remind me that you're greater than all my fears. You're stronger than all my hardships. You're more powerful than any temptation. I can lean on your strength to guide me and uphold me. When life is tough, you call me to have fortitude in the face of my fears, to do right no matter how daunting the task may seem. I know that you'll be right there by my side, providing the grace I need.

God, grant me the power to move when I'm standing still, to act when I want to ignore, to fight when I want to give in. Teach me how to rely on your grace and practice virtue in the everyday moments of my life, even when it's hard. Help me face my fears, and give me the grace to step out in fortitude.

Amen.

On My Heart

_____

_____

_____

_____

_____

_____

_____

Becoming_____

_____

_____

_____

_____

The Virtue of Fortitude

From Fear to Fortitude

"Oh no, I can't go in there." I bent over, resting my hands on my knees, to take deep, calming breaths. My family had met up with a group of friends for an epic hike to the ice caves in New York. As we descended the steep, rocky stairs, the sky began to close in above us. Sunlight had been streaming through a thin crack at the top of the crevice, glistening on the water that trickled from cracks in the rock. It was glorious.

Yet, this bend, this descent into the dark unknown, was too much for my nerves. I peered into the dark cavern, not knowing what would be ahead. Fear gripped my chest and weakened my knees. It was fear of the unknown.

My hiking crew had a good chuckle, and began encouraging me: "You can't go back now! Come on, I'll be right with you. You can do this!" Someone grabbed my hand for encouragement, and leaning on them for support, I stepped into that dimly lit cave, and, finally back out again. Each new obstacle brought with it a new wave of fear: the bridge over the pitch-black abyss, the crawl space that closed in on all sides of me, the thin crevice I had to squeeze through, side-stepping to fit between the unforgiving face of the rocks.

However, each new obstacle also brought with it another chance to conquer that fear. An opportunity to lean on the help of others, put one foot in front of another, and step out in faith that I would get through this—as had every hiker before me. Courage doesn't come without fear. Rather, it's a response to fear; courage can only be practiced in the presence of the things we're afraid of.

Holy Courage

Fortitude is the virtue of courage in moral matters. It "ensures firmness in difficulties and constancy in the pursuit of the good" (*Catechism*, 1808). Fortitude isn't a virtue for when life is easy, but for when it's most challenging. There's nothing special about doing right when everyone else is doing right, nothing heroic about choosing good when there's no sacrifice involved.

When things get hard, that's when we need this virtue. In the face of temptations, obstacles, and fears, holy courage helps us endure the difficulties of life. Like the human bravery and courage I needed to take that first wavering footstep into the dark cave, fortitude helps us step out into the darkness, to move forward when difficulty crosses our path. But unlike human courage, fortitude is *moral* courage. When I faced my fear of the unknown in my hike, I leaned on the encouragement and strength of the friends surrounding me. When we face our spiritual fears and challenges, God is our strength; he gives us encouragement and the power to get through every difficulty.

Fortitude Every Day

Fortitude is another one of those virtues for martyrs. The *Catechism* says that martyrdom is the greatest act of fortitude. The martyrs rely on this virtue to face the greatest fear of all—the fear of death, for the sake of the truth and the kingdom of God: "He endures death through an act of fortitude" (*Catechism*, 2473). Once again, we see how great virtue isn't limited to great sacrifice.

The martyrs faced death, but before that, they faced the trials of living the faith in daily life. They were committed to standing strong in doing the difficult right thing in small ways every day. How do we know that? Because human life is filled daily with small trials and myriad opportunities to practice virtue. Every time we exercise any virtue, we call on the virtue of fortitude.

Face Your Fears

When we wake up in the morning, we have so many choices: hit the snooze button, roll over, get out of bed and grump around, reach for the coffee. There are so many things that are easier to do in the morning than pray, things that require less effort than being thankful for the day God gave us. Fear can hold us back from facing our day, but fortitude helps us to lean on God for our strength from the moment we pry our eyes open. It helps us get out of bed and energizes us to prayerfully dedicate our day to God.

When we're with a group of friends and gossip takes the reins in the conversation, it's easier to join in than to bow out. We even rational-ize it in our heads sometimes by saying we're joking or that it's all in good fun, but, in our hearts, we know that it's wrong. Fear often holds us back from changing the subject or even backing out of the conversation. We don't want to be a killjoy or a "Debbie Downer." We're afraid of others' opinions: What will they say about *us* later on? Fortitude can help us do the right thing in spite of fear. It can give us the strength to go against the crowd and be charitable in our speech.

Another example of everyday fortitude is in maintaining our relation-ships. It's hard to make time to call a friend. It's exhausting to constant-ly invest in disciplining our kids. We'd rather do something relaxing at the end of the day than do something kind for our spouse. We may even resent the interruption in our day when it's time to pray or go to Mass. We're often so invested in our own goals and to-do list that we're afraid we're going to lose our time or some part of ourselves by serving and loving others. Relationships aren't easy. They require time and attention, sacrifice, and risk. It's scary to put ourselves out there, wondering if our love will be validated and returned.

Look to the Cross

As Christians, we look to the cross. Jesus loved us without holding back. He loved us to the end. Even knowing that many would reject his love, he still willingly made the sacrifice of giving his life out of love for us. It wasn't an easy thing to do. Jesus showed us a great example of fortitude for our relationships by embracing his cross despite his fears, with full knowledge of the pain it would cause him. He leaned on the Father for strength and calls us to do the same.

Fortitude allows us to pick up our cross and do the hard thing. It allows us to be vulnerable and put ourselves out there in love for others. It helps us practice everyday virtue, whether it's getting out of bed and praying, avoiding gossip, fighting temptation, witnessing to the faith, or simply living as a Catholic woman on fire with love for God in all the little things. For any fear we encounter, any difficulty we come up against in living out our faith, fortitude is the virtue that enables us to do the right thing. Relying on God's grace and strength, we can face all our fears.

An Invitation to Ponder

What are some of the difficulties of daily life that require you to practice the virtue of fortitude? How can you do the right thing in the face of these hardships? How can you turn to the cross for inspiration and strength in these times of trial and temptation?

_____

_____

_____

_____

_____

_____

_____

_____

_____

_____

_____

Connecting to Scripture

PRAYER TO THE HOLY SPIRIT BEFORE READING SCRIPTURE

Come, Holy Spirit. Fill me with every grace and blessing necessary to understand the message prepared for and awaiting me in the Scriptures. May I grow deeper in faith, in hope, and in love with Jesus as I spend this time with the Word of God. Amen.

⌐ Matthew 10:26–31 _____

_____

_____

⌐ Mark 10:35–40 _____

_____

_____

⌐ Mark 14:32–42 _____

_____

_____

🖎 Romans 8:31–39 _____

_____

_____

🖎 1 Peter 4:12–13 _____

_____

_____

Scripture Reflection

The Cup

Sometimes, the audacity of the apostles leaves me shaking my head. In Mark 10, the apostles James and John got ahead of themselves big time: "[Jesus], we want you to do for us whatever we ask of you" (Mark 10:35). Giggle, snort. Okay, let's see what they want. "Grant us to sit, one at your right hand and one at your left, in your glory" (Mark 10:37).

I can just imagine the look on Jesus' face: Hah, okay, guys; let's be real here. He warned them that they didn't know what they were talking about and that a reward that big comes with a hefty price: "Are you able to drink the cup that I drink... ?" (Mark 10:38). James and John may have realized at this point they had overstepped, but they couldn't back down. They couldn't look like wimps in front of the other guys, so they gave a resounding, "Yeah, sure. We can do it."

They didn't know what they were up against. They didn't realize the extent of Jesus' suffering. At this point, they were excited about his kingdom and wanted to make sure they got a piece of the glory. While Jesus didn't promise them the positions of power they asked for, he did promise them they would drink the cup—that they would share in his suffering. But they didn't yet understand what that meant.

Before Jesus was arrested, tried, tortured, and crucified, he took his disciples out to a deserted garden. He asked most of them to stay a little distance away, but selected a few disciples to go with him while he withdrew to pray. Who would the chosen three be? Peter, of course, the rock, the leader. But also James and John, the two who were promised to "share the cup." Now was the time for Jesus to reveal to them what he meant by that.

We hear him pray, "Father, for you all things are possible; remove this cup from me; yet not what I want, but what you want" (Mark 14:36). This was the signal to James and John: Here it comes; this is what's in store for you. Notice that Jesus was afraid. James and John were all macho when they agreed to drink the cup, but Jesus was distressed; he was filled with fear. He understood the horror of what was to come. He didn't *want* it, but he would *accept* it if it was the Father's will.

Fortitude in the Face of Fear

James and John had made a show of enthusiastically accepting the cup. They hid their fear. Jesus, on the other hand, was visibly troubled, distressed, and sorrowful unto death. He was obviously afraid.

In the garden, Jesus showed us that it's okay to be afraid. Fear is a natural, healthy, human response to suffering. It gives us a heads-up that there's something difficult coming. Jesus demonstrated that fear for the apostles. He felt every shiver of fear, every tremble of anxiety. It rocked him, physically, so much that one of the Gospel accounts even mentions him sweating blood.

Jesus didn't let that fear control him. He turned to God in prayer, begging the Father to uphold him. Jesus submitted himself to the Father's will, even though he was afraid, in acceptance of all that was required of him. From that moment on, we see how Jesus demonstrated strength and fortitude throughout his entire Passion. He endured the scourging without making a sound, he stood in front of a throng demanding his death, he embraced his cross and carried it along the long road, and he hung three long hours upon it before handing over his spirit. In his last moments, he cried out in prayer again, reminding us that the Father's strength was with him through it all.

Fortitude isn't the absence of fear; it's strength in spite of fear. Jesus showed us how this virtue turns us to God in prayer in times of distress. Like Jesus in the garden, we can cry out to God whenever suffering comes our way. We can admit that we're afraid. It's even okay to ask God to take the suffering away from us. If Jesus did it, then we can too. But we also must be ready to accept suffering if that's God's will. Jesus calls us time and again to "take up our crosses" and follow him. We accept it in a humble way though. Unlike James and John, who accepted the cup with bravado in front of their peers, we are called to accept the cup like Jesus, with willing resignation to the will of the Father.

Share in Christ's Suffering

Peter was there when James and John accepted the cup. He was there in the garden when Jesus revealed the level of suffering which that cup entailed. He connected the dots: "Beloved, do not be surprised at the fiery ordeal that is taking place among you to test you, as though something strange were happening to you. But rejoice insofar as you are sharing Christ's sufferings, so that you may also be glad and shout for joy when his glory is revealed" (1 Peter 4:12, 13).

Suffering is a natural part of the Christian life. If we try to live holy and virtuous lives, we're going to face our share of obstacles for the sake of the faith. It's going to be hard along the way. We're going to be persecuted for our beliefs, for trying to do the right thing. We're going to run up against daunting and difficult tasks. It's natural to be afraid, troubled, and distressed.

When things are going well, we might be a little haughty, like James and John. We might have a bring-it-on attitude. But when trouble hits, we might feel more like Jesus: Take this cup away from me. Peter linked our acceptance of suffering back to James and John's desire for glory. It's through suffering that God's glory is revealed. If we want a share in the glory, we need to accept our share in the suffering. We need to endure the cross to get to the Resurrection.

Have Courage

So have courage. Not because there's nothing to be afraid of, but because Christ has gone ahead of us. He has suffered all, endured all, for our sake. We can unite all our crosses—big or small—to his suffering. We can turn to the Father in prayer as Jesus did. Draw your strength from him. He can conquer our fears; he can overcome them.

With fortitude, we can endure all things and persevere to the end despite all our fears.

An Invitation to Share

1. For James and John, suffering took them by surprise. They should have known it was coming because Jesus prophesied it many times, but they didn't. Peter tells us not to be surprised by suffering. What's your outlook on suffering? Do you anticipate it? Or are you in denial until it hits? Which of these Gospel characters do you most identify with?

_____

_____

_____

_____

_____

_____

_____

_____

_____

_____

_____

2. Jesus showed us that fear is a human response to suffering, but at the same time, taught us to respond to suffering with prayer and acceptance of God's will. How can you practice the virtue of fortitude in responding to fear more like Jesus?

3. In Romans 8:35-39, Paul makes an extensive list of the difficult things in life. But he concludes by saying that none of these things can separate us from the love of Christ. What difficult things have you endured, or are you enduring now? How can you remind yourself of God's love even in the midst of all this suffering?

Closing Prayer

My Jesus, sometimes it's hard for me to accept the fear and suffering that come into my life. I want to wish it all away. But in your agony in the garden, you give an example of how to respond to trials in life. You show me that fear is nothing to be ashamed of; it's a natural part of my human nature. You show me that there's nothing wrong with an aversion to suffering, or even praying for suffering to go away. It gives me comfort that you felt my fear, that you understand my prayer.

Help me respond to fear as you did. You leaned on the Father for fortitude and strength. You turned to him in a time of devoted prayer. Give me the grace to follow your example. Help me lift my eyes and heart to you in prayer and rely on you to get me through. May I always pick up my cross and follow you.

Lord, I know that the cross is an inevitable part of life. I know that, as a Christian, you call me to submit to the Father's will in all things. And I also know that it's natural for me to feel afraid. When fear and suffering strike, give me the virtue of fortitude. Help me to do the right thing no matter what obstacles stand in my way. Help me persevere through temptation, persecution, suffering, fear, and all adversity. With fortitude, nothing can separate me from your love.

Amen.

Lord, I pray for

Fortitude

The Gift of Invitation:
7 Ways That Jesus Invites You to a Life of Grace
(Stay Connected Journals for Catholic Women #1)

By Allison Gingras

You're invited to something wonderful — a more abundant life and a closer relationship with God — all you need to do is respond.

In **The Gift of Invitation: 7 Ways Jesus Invites You to a Life of Grace**, you will:

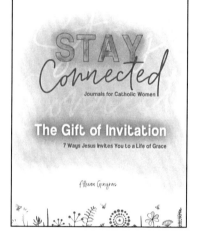

- Discover the seven powerful invitations Jesus extends to you, including the invitation to follow him, forgive from your heart, and know his Father's many gifts

- Explore the Bible to develop a deeper relationship with Jesus

- See how each invitation plays out in your own life

- Reflect on how you can be better prepared to accept Jesus' invitations.

Perfect for individual or group study, the seven chapters includes reflections and scripture, with space for journaling.

Exploring the Catholic Classics:
How Spiritual Reading Can Help You Grow in Wisdom
(Stay Connected Journals for Catholic Women #2)

By Tiffany Walsh

The Catholic classics are full of wisdom, advice, and inspiration to enrich the lives of modern women, and **Exploring the Catholic Classics** is a great way to access that wisdom and apply it to your life.

In **Exploring the Catholic Classics**, you will:

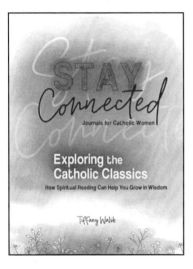

• Learn about seven inspiring historical and modern works of Catholic literature

• Read selected passages from the writings of St. Thérèse of Lisieux, Pope St. John Paul II, St. Francis de Sales, Thomas á Kempis, and more

• Study these spiritual works in light of the Scriptures

• Reflect on significant spiritual themes and chronicle your own thoughts and experiences

Perfect for individual or group study, the seven chapters includes reflections and scripture, with space for journaling.

Invite the Holy Spirit into Your Life:
Growing in Love, Joy, Peace, Patience, Patience, Kindness, Goodness, Faithfulness, Gentleness, and Self-Control
(Stay Connected Journals for Catholic Women #3)

By Deanna Bartalini

"The fruit of the Spirit is love, joy, peace, patience, kindness, generosity, faithfulness, gentleness, and self-control," St. Paul wrote to the Galatians. "If we live by the Spirit, let us also be guided by the Spirit" (Galatians 5:22–23, 25). Those words are just as relevant and powerful for you today as they were for the Galatians.

In **Invite the Holy Spirit into Your Life**, you will:

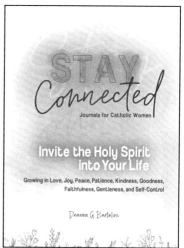

- Learn the life-changing power of the fruits of the Holy Spirit

- Explore each fruit through real-life stories, Scripture, and Church teachings

- Examine how you are cultivating the fruits of the Spirit in your own life

Perfect for individual or group study, the seven chapters includes reflections and scripture, with space for journaling.